KEEP YOURSELF ALIVE

KEEP YOUR SELF ALIVE

| A 21st CENTURY GUIDE TO PERFECT HEALTH AND FREEDOM FROM STRESS

Roger G. Lanphear

unified PUBLICATIONS
Knowledge for the Twenty-First Century
1050 University Avenue, Suite 103
San Diego, California 92103

Copyright © 1992 by Roger G. Lanphear

All rights reserved

No part of this book may be reproduced in any form or by any electronic or mechanical means, including information storage and retrieval systems, without permission in writing from the publisher, except by a reviewer, who may quote brief passages in a review. Published by

unified PUBLICATIONS
1050 University Avenue, Suite 103
San Diego, California 92103

ISBN: 0-9625800-2-3

Printed in the United States of America

Preface

There is no doubt in my mind that this is knowledge of the highest order. Over the course of twenty years, these techniques to access the infinite energies of creation were revealed to me. I had no idea I was weaving together such complete and simple systems.

I know by my own life that these pages expose profound Truth. They work for me and for the people I've shared them with. This is knowledge, the likes of which can shatter archaic notions about what is human.

I wrote this book the same way I wrote three others. Without an outline, chapter headings, or even a list of topics, I sat in a quiet spot in a park, accessed wisdom with this technology, and wrote down the words that came. The book unfolded for me, as it will for you—logically, completely, and easily.

In fact, you can write a book the same way. These Master Systems cultivate perfect health that unlocks All-Knowing Intelligence. It only takes time and perseverence.

That is the key—time and perseverence. Then all that you are is yours to experience. And isn't that what perfect health and freedom from stress really are?

ROGER LANPHEAR

CONTENTS

THE GOAL   1

PART I

THE BASIC TOOLS

KNOW THY SELF   11
Understanding the purpose of life and realizing what "Your Attributes" are

THE ATONEMENT   18
Learning the fundamental technique to transform your life

CLAIMING ALL-KNOWING INTELLIGENCE   25
Unifying consciously with the order of almighty nature

PART II

LAYING THE FOUNDATION

BEING A CREATOR   35
Mastering techniques to clean up conscious and subconscious thoughts—the basis for creating

COMMON CONSCIOUSNESS   42
Identifying false beliefs held by society and correcting them

COMING TO GRIPS WITH FEAR   49
Erasing illusions that produce fear and substituting a reality that is safe and supportive

TAPPING ALL-KNOWING INTELLIGENCE   56
Turning on your automatic guidance system to process information and lead you safety

ANGER MELTDOWN   62
Administering the antidote to neutralize anger so you can respond appropriately to disturbances

THE UNIFIED FIELD   69
Learning Truth and feeling love with expanded awareness of the most elementary ingredient in creation

CULTIVATING LOVE   76
Opening up to the healing power of giving and receiving love with a simple formula

PART III

STRESS MANAGEMENT

BODY CONSCIOUSNESS   85
Managing the individual forms of life in your body and understanding how your body fits into the scheme of nature

COMMUNICATING WITH YOUR BODY   90
Listening to your body to learn its needs

NEUTRALIZING GLOBAL STRESS   97
Mopping up negativism resulting from ignorance, wars, turmoil, and planetary abuse

ILLNESS AND DEATH   103
Healing outside of time and accepting the role of death

PART IV

THE REWARDS

WISDOM 111
Strengthening your ties to universal Truth by receiving solutions to your problems

KNOWLEDGE FROM THE MASTERS 118
Listening to the wisdom and feeling the love from Masters such as Jesus, Buddha, Krishna, Babaji, and Mohammed

PEACE 124
Instilling inner peace and splashing that peace into the environment for a new world order

ABUNDANCE 130
Manifesting wealth in a way that provides for your needs while supporting the highest good of everyone and the planet

IDEAL RELATIONSHIPS 135
Allowing the perfect and most supportive people into your personal and business life

HAPPINESS 140
Grounding happiness as a never-ending feeling that underlies all emotion and activity

LIGHT 143
Radiating Truth for all to see by your mere presence

YOUR JOURNAL OF TRUTH 145
Writing knowledge relevant for this time, this place, and your state of consciousness

TECHNIQUES

YOUR ATTRIBUTES	17
DISCOVERING THE ATONEMENT VIBRATION	24
THE ATONEMENT	24
CONSTANTLY MARVEL	30
DISCOVERING "YES" AND "NO" TOOLS	31
ENLIVENING YOUR POWER	40
MONITORING THOUGHTS	41
CORRECTING SUBCONSCIOUS THOUGHTS	41
CORRECTING COMMON CONSCIOUSNESS	48
REDUCING FEAR	55
BREATHING TECHNIQUES FOR FEAR AND ANGER	68
ANGER MELTDOWN	68
LEARNING TRUTH	75
FEELING LOVE	75
THE LOVE CONNECTION	82

MAKING LOVE	82
THE LOVE MELTDOWN	82
BODY MANAGEMENT	89
DISCOVERING YOUR BODY SIGNAL	95
LISTENING TO YOUR BODY	96
THE PERFECT HEALTH VIBRATION	108
HEALING SPECIFIC ILLNESS	108
ACCESSING WISDOM	117
CONNECTING WITH THE MASTERS	124
MANIFESTING WEALTH	134
THE RELATIONSHIP VIBRATION	139
THE JOURNAL OF TRUTH	147

CHAPTER ONE

The Goal

Keep yourself alive. That was the goal for managing stress and health in the twentieth century. It is narrow and short sighted.

Keep your Self alive. Those are twenty-first century words. They introduce the true you—your Self—which is strong, infinite, and powerfully in charge, instead of finite, frail, and a victim of circumstances.

In the twentieth century you limited yourself. In the twenty-first century you accept your Self which is greater than the greatest you can imagine.

This book teaches you how to awaken and keep your Self alive. These techniques are not the only path, but they are easy and simple. One thing is certain. Techniques to enliven the Self will one day be practiced by everyone to gain perfect health and eliminate the debilitating toll of stress. What you are about to learn is cutting-edge technology.

A conscious Self enlivens every aspect of life, and this knowledge can be studied from many perspectives, such as prosperity and money making or even relationships and sex. In these pages the wisdom is presented to reach the goal of perfect health and freedom from stress. At the same time all other aspects of life improve.

Health is a two edged sword. Everything you do leaves its imprint on your health. Conversely, everything you do is either limited or enhanced by your health. So important is your health that all your actions are intertwined with it. Whether you just need to complete a school assignment, or whether you want to tackle a life purpose, health is a silent partner.

Too often in spiritual circles the physical body is put down. Sometimes it is even renounced. "I am not my body. I am a spirit, so I disclaim the physical. I rise above it. I will not allow it to influence me in the slightest."

Have you heard that? Of course. Maybe you've even said it. On the road to accepting immortality and spirituality as fact, some people go through a period of denouncing the importance of the physical body. They somehow think that spirit can only manifest when they have given up all that is physical.

Well, the time has now come to grow into full Self-realization while recognizing and nourishing the physical aspect of your Self.

If your physical body were not important, you wouldn't have it. Indeed, if the physical world weren't important, you wouldn't be in it. Nothing in creation is senseless. All of it has a beautiful connection to everything else. Every aspect of your world is a stitch in the fabric of creation. Every stitch is necessary and beautiful. Each stitch is perfect.

A very important—nay, necessary—aspect of you is your body. Although it is only present on earth for this time, it is a necessary part of your total being while you're here.

That doesn't mean that when you drop your body, you will be less of a total being. Each time

The Goal

you go through the change called death or birth, the bundle of conscious energy that is "you" takes on a specific form with a certain vibration. The form you take has infinite possibilities, depending on where in creation you are and what you want to accomplish.

Right now you are on earth, and you are here for some particular purpose. You may have a sense of why you're here, or you may be searching. It doesn't matter. The fact is that you have a physical body that greatly influences your life while you're here.

No amount of denial of the importance of your body can change that. No dose of spirituality can change that. You have a body, and that body is a necessary aspect of who you are now and what you do here on earth.

From time to time Masters demonstrate so-called super-normal feats. They walk on water, levitate, manifest gems, and so on. These are meant to demonstrate the connection of body, mind, and spirit. Unfortunately, the feats are often misunderstood. Many people view the demonstrations as proof the physical body is meaningless baggage. That is neither Truth nor the Master's purpose.

These demonstrations come from people who use their body at its highest potential. That requires a body in perfect health. Full potential can only be demonstrated by people operating in wholeness: a healthy body, a healthy mind, and a healthy spirit. The three are intertwined, and all three are necessary to reach perfection.

To be one hundred percent successful in everything you do, you need the help and support of a perfectly healthy body. In a very true sense it is the foundation for reaching all your goals.

That is why the techniques in this book are perhaps the most spiritual practices you can do. They lead to perfect health—the foundation for all your spiritual awakenings.

Your physical body is not an island unto itself. It is a part of your Self, which is far more beautiful, far more extensive, far more complicated, yet far simpler than you can imagine. Whatever you do effects every other aspect of your being. The health of your physical body has a direct bearing on your mind and spirit.

Many of the techniques in this book seem to have nothing to do with the body, but the body is effected. Likewise, many of the techniques don't seem to be spiritual, yet the spirit is forever elevated. You can't move one leg of a chair without moving the entire chair. Every part of that chair feels a tug. Body, mind, and spirit are all elevated when any one of them is improved.

The human body is specially designed by creative intelligence to bring you the experience of life on earth. You have the five sense organs to comprehend the many forms that exist at this level of vibration in this corner of creation. That same human body is not designed for experiencing life in another star system, or even another planet of our sun. It is uniquely formulated for the earth experience.

That does not mean you are restricted to this planet. Quite the contrary. You are capable of experiencing each and every corner of the entire cosmos. When you go to another corner, you manifest a local body to help with the experience. That is all you've done here. You

The Goal

took on a local physical body so life on earth at this time could be meaningful.

Now that you have a human earth body, you are locked into this time and space. You are in touch with the plants, animals, terrain, and elements of this planet. This is your playpen, your class room, your auditorium, and your home. It is also your connection to all the rest of creation, even the connection to Our Creator. Everything you need to fully appreciate who you are and how you fit into the scheme of life is right here on earth now.

Thanks to your physical body you can perceive in this lifetime your connection to All. Right here, now, you can appreciate and feel the perfection of creation and know how you fit into it. That, dear friends, is enlightenment. It the goal of every life, and you can experience enlightenment in this life with your present body.

In a hologram a 3-D picture appears when a laser light is passed through a special film cylinder. Amazingly, when you snip off a bit of the film, make another cylinder with the piece, and pass the laser light through it, the same 3-D image reappears. The entire blueprint of the image is embedded in even the smallest bit of the film. It is the same here on earth. The blueprint of the entire cosmos is here for you to discover. You don't have to travel to far away galaxies to unlock nature's mysteries. They are all here to unearth.

That is why you must give attention to your health. In this lifetime you have all you need to perceive the 3-D picture of creation. Your life is a snip of creation. As such your life can reveal the entire scheme of creation, just like a snip of the hologram film reveals its entire picture.

In order to fathom creation, you must perceive with the accuracy your body is designed to give. Your body is your vehicle of perception, so the body must be running at peak performance. It must be stress-free—in perfect health.

To live on earth at this time without perceiving the entire cosmos is wasting your life. It is throwing away your body, like selling a diamond for the price of spinach.

Don't ever lose sight of that fact. You have the chance and the ability in this lifetime to realize your connection to the entire cosmos, but you need a stress-free body to do it.

Enlightenment—living in full the experiences creation has to offer—is so important that all the magical energies of the universe are at your fingertips to help. It only takes your dogged determination to cultivate the perfect health of a stress-free body.

To have perfect health is to be stress-free. The two go together. It means your body is free of abnormalities, and it also means you aren't overwhelmed by a stressed environment.

The assaults on your body from a world of pollution, angry people, pressures, deadlines, and heartbreaks tear down your tissues, nerves, and immune system. The outcome is heart disease, ulcers, tension, and nearly all known maladies. With sickness you cope even less with your environment, leading to more illness. The problems compound. Stress builds upon itself. A vicious cycle seems never-ending.

This is what nearly everyone experiences. It is no wonder that illness is considered inevitable, stress is viewed as normal, and perfect health is

The Goal

<u>believed to be impossible.</u> Well, perfect health is achievable. Stress is not necessary.

The goal for this course is for you to have a physical body with all of its systems functioning at peak efficiency. The goal is for you to react calmly and lovingly to your environment without inducing illness or damaging it. This is perfect health. This is being stress free. This is enlightenment. There can be no higher goal in life.

Without stress, your body is a precious gem. A healthy body is a clear diamond, reflecting your True nature. It is the perfect vehicle for a life of fun, learning, and achievement.

PART I

THE BASIC TOOLS

CHAPTER TWO

Know Thy Self

Perfect health is a natural condition. The first step toward perfect health is to know that. Knowing is the key. You must know and accept the naturalness of perfect health for it to be in your life.

This might sound strange. If perfect health is natural, then how could knowing it have any bearing? The answer lies in your very nature. You are made in the image of Our Creator. That means that all the attributes of the creative energies and intelligence underlying creation are also yours. They include the power to create.

Yes, you are a creator in the most basic, elementary sense. You have the power to muster the energies of creation to create your world, your experiences.

This does not mean you are just a potential creator. You are already, in this moment, a creator. You don't need to evolve higher. You need to learn nothing. You already have all the knowledge, all the tools, and all the ingredients to create. You are an expert at it. You have done it from day one, and you have never stopped creating. The process is already one hundred percent efficient.

PART I / The Basic Tools

Creating begins with a thought. A simple thought musters all the creative forces to manifest what the thought represents.

That is why knowing who and what you are is of paramount importance. What you think about yourself—and your Self—is your experience. Think you are frail, vulnerable, weak, or sickly, and you experience frailty, vulnerability, weakness, or sickness. Your ability to be a creator is so powerful, it can override, overshadow, and cover up your own perfect nature, and that is precisely what most people do. Then they find it nearly impossible to grasp who and what they really are.

Oddly, the condition people find themselves in is actually proof of their perfection. They are living proof that they do create what they believe. They believe sickness is an inevitable condition, so it is inevitable. They believe they are vulnerable to accidents, diseases, and stress, so they suffer. They believe they have limited strengths, so they experience weakness.

It's a catch-22. The more they believe they're weak, the weaker they become. And on it goes.

Their experience of what they think is so complete that they no longer see the cause-effect relationship. Weakness seems to be their nature. Disease and injuries appear to be random, arbitrary, and natural. They have dwelled so long on these mistakes that they think they are observing the natural scheme of life.

Well, you are made in the image of Our Creator. Call that God, or intelligence, or life force, or nature, or whatever. The name is not important. Our Creator's Attributes, however, are important because they are the basis for what you are.

Know Thy Self

Our Creator is greater than the entire cosmos. Our Creator is smaller than the most elementary particle. Our Creator is more powerful than the big bang, yet more silent than nothingness. Within Our Creator lies the potential for all the multifarious forms in creation—all the life forms, the entire spectrum of energies, and the trillions of chemical compounds in an ever-expanding universe.

Within each form resides the blueprint of Our Creator, like the sliver of the hologram film having the entire picture. Nothing is ever separated from Our Creator. Within each form, whether a single atom or galaxy or whether a single cell or your Self, there resides the blueprint of Our Creator.

When you know this, you open yourself to the Truth of who and what you are. What you expect and believe changes. Instead of being weak and frail, you are strong. Instead of disease, you experience perfect health. The process is automatic. By simply knowing you are made in the image of Our Creator, you change your thoughts about your own attributes. That knowledge alone improves what you create, what you experience.

That is why you must *know* who and what you are. It is the first step in your journey toward perfect health.

Everyone has an idea of what attributes Our Creator has. Some of these are indeed Truth. However, others are flavored with superstition and myth. Many people believe Our Creator is to be feared. Others see "Him" with human frailties of jealousy, revenge, or vindictiveness. Some visualize a demanding being with strict codes of right and wrong, sitting in judgment.

PART I / The Basic Tools

Those images of Our Creator are far from the Truth. It is not the blueprint of the image from which you are made.

Before you can experience perfect health, you must firmly ingrain the Truth of who and what you are into your consciousness. You do this by thinking attributes of Our Creator and accepting them as your own. This is your first technique.

As you think each of the following attributes, be aware of the meaning that follows. Think them at least once each day, at any time it is most natural. Perhaps you have a few moments after the alarm goes off in the morning. Maybe you can think them as you commute to work. It is best to do this technique the same time each day so you can get a routine going. However, the important point is to think the attributes each and every day, regardless of when. The knowledge of "Your Attributes" is the backbone for all your other thoughts.

I am made in the image of Our Creator. Therefore I am Love. Love is a feeling of belonging. It is feeling unified with another being, any other creature, or any aspect of creation. You are connected to all parts of creation, and that connection is felt as love.

Therefore I am Light. Your own existence is proof of order and perfection. By opening yourself up to your own intelligence, you become a beacon of Truth so others can realize their own worth.

Therefore I am Happiness, Joy, and Bliss. This is the state of mind you are created to experience. There is no need for a life of turmoil, fear, tension, or sadness. These come about when you forget your true nature. Think of a forest or a flower garden. Could those plants,

14

Know Thy Self

streams, and animals be created from sadness? No. They exemplify joy and they exude bliss because that is the nature of Our Creator.

Therefore I am All-Knowing Intelligence. The order of nature is undeniable. From the four seasons to the chemical reactions, you live in a precise and orderly world. It is not random, yet it is infinitely complex. Clearly, that is intelligence, and you are of that intelligence. It permeates you, and you have total access to it. You can know anything you need to know.

Therefore I am Present Everywhere For All Time. You are more than your physical body whose main purpose is to lock you into this time and this planet. But, time and matter are not what they appear to be. Time is a function of speed, and matter is really just energy, and they are all made up of what Einstein called The Unified Field. The Unified Field is your true, ultimate body, and it is present everywhere for all time.

Therefore I am Perfection. Our Creator does not create imperfections. That is why science can rely on prediction and orderliness. Whatever happens has a reason which stems from the perfect flow of energy. Anything that appears imperfect is simply evidence of incomplete knowledge, a misunderstanding.

Therefore I am Peace and Gentleness. Underlying the dynamic activity around you is peace. When you feel it within, it is your foundation for strength. Gentleness is power. It is the anchor for all the forms and expressions of nature.

Therefore I am Infinite Energy. All that is around you is energy. All the forms you see and hear are but expressions of energy. Even the

PART I / The Basic Tools

entire cosmos is just a sliver of never-ending energy. You are that infinite energy. It is your dutiful servant.

Therefore I am a Creator. You can stir the ethers of the unmanifest to create your own world of experiences. Our Creator could not give you less than He/She has, you are loved so much. The building blocks to create any experience are yours for the asking. Just be certain you want what you ask for. Our Creator only knows "YES."

Therefore I am Abundance. This naturally follows. Since you encompass a range from peace to infinite energy, you manifest your own world of abundance. The degree to which you do so depends on your own expectations, beliefs, and desires.

Therefore am Without Judgment. People sometimes think they are being judged by Our Creator. They even speak of a judgment day. Any judgment is simply the interplay of cause and effect. There is no intermediary step called judgment. Our Creator gave you the power to create anything. Just set up the cause, and the effect comes without judgment. Every person has that power, and it must be respected. Allow everyone else to create their own world. Don't judge them or their creations because Our Creator doesn't judge you or your creations.

All of these attributes are explored in depth in the following chapters. There's no need to fully grasp the meanings now. The short explanations are only hints of the knowledge underlying these affirmations. The important and only point is to think these attributes for yourself each day. It lays a solid foundation in your thoughts to manifest perfect health without stress.

Know Thy Self

YOUR ATTRIBUTES

I am made in the image of Our Creator. Therefore I am Love.

I am made in the image of Our Creator. Therefore I am Light.

I am made in the image of Our Creator. Therefore I am Happiness, Joy, and Bliss.

I am made in the image of Our Creator. Therefore I am All-Knowing Intelligence.

I am made in the image of Our Creator. Therefore I am Present Everywhere For All Time.

I am made in the image of Our Creator. Therefore I am Perfection.

I am made in the image of Our Creator. Therefore I am Peace and Gentleness.

I am made in the image of Our Creator. Therefore I am Infinite Energy.

I am made in the image of Our Creator. Therefore I am a Creator.

I am made in the image of Our Creator. Therefore I am Abundance.

I am made in the image of Our Creator. Therefore I am Without Judgment.

CHAPTER THREE

The Atonement

"Your Attributes" are not wishful thinking. These are not traits for you to strive to develop. They are already yours. At this moment you embody every attribute, and there are no prerequisites for having them. Indeed, there is nothing you can do to lose them.

You are made in the image of Our Creator. The act is complete. You are already completely created. Our Creator did not put together your ingredients in a bowl to be baked later, like a cake. The cake is finished—luscious, light batter filled with fruit and nuts, topped with rich frosting and gorgeously decorated. You are all that Our Creator is, and you are all that now!

You could not have been made any other way. Our Creator feels more love for you than you can imagine. Think of a moment in your life when you felt so much love for someone you wanted to climb to the top of a building and shout your love to the world below. Then multiply that feeling by infinity. That is the love Our Creator feels for you.

Would you want your children to have less than you? How ludicrous it would be to think that you always want to be better than your sons and daughters, or to be more capable, or to possess more comforts, or to be healthier. A

The Atonement

loving parent could not entertain such thoughts. If anything, you want your children to have more than you, not less. If you feel that way with the love you have for your children, how could Our Creator give you less than He/She has?

Our Creator is more than the greatest expanse of Creation. And so are you. Our Creator is less than the smallest particle—smaller than the least vibration. And so are you. There is no place Our Creator does not exist; omnipresence is the reality. And so it is for you. Our Creator is mightier than all the energy of the cosmos, yet Our Creator is more silent than absolute vacuum. The same is true for you. All that Our Creator is you are also. And that means *All*. You are loved so much, it could not be otherwise.

You can deny it, and that is your option. You see, along with all "Your Attributes" comes freewill and the responsibility to manage your own life. No-one—not even Our Creator—will ever take that from you. It is a precious quality that you can never abdicate. The experiences you create for yourself are your responsibility.

So, while you are made in the image of Our Creator, you can create a reality that appears to deny your status. What would you say of a strong and healthy billionaire who thinks he is penniless and dying of cancer? You'd say he is suffering from a delusion. That is precisely the sad reality on earth right now. Most people are suffering from delusions.

They think they are only a physical body. They think they are victims of disease, poverty, and weakness. They think they are alone, unloved, and unwanted. That is not the Truth.

The entire creation is actually your full whole body. You share that body—creation—with

PART I / The Basic Tools

everyone and with Our Creator while retaining uniqueness. This is such precious Truth. With it you can understand why there is unity along with infinite variations. Diversity, yet unity. Unity, yet diversity. That is the divine scheme.

Since each unique person within the unity of the cosmos has freewill, everyone is free to think and create at will. The whole range of thoughts and manifestations is possible. That includes denying your existence, denying "Your Attributes," and denying your status. It may sound strange that a king would deny a kingdom, but that is exactly what so many people do.

So powerful are you that even denials bring about the experiences you expect. Deny your attribute of existing in unity with the entire cosmos, and you experience loneliness, claustrophobia, limitations, boundaries, and oppression. Deny your true status, and you cut off the feeling and unifying forces of love.

※ <u>Thinking daily "Your Attributes" reverses the denial. It affirms what you want to believe. Above all, it lays out what you want to experience in your daily activity. It is a perfect beginning.</u>

The next techniques are designed to crack open the subconscious levels of your mind to lay the foundation for perfect health—and a whole lot more. The techniques are simple, but you must tackle each one before moving on.

That is a strong command: you must tackle each technique. Yes, but they aren't hard, and anyone can do them. Anyone. That means everyone, including you. <u>It requires only a little bit of tenacity—a stick-to-itiveness.</u> Just be conscientious, and perfect health with freedom from stress is inevitable.

The Atonement

The fundamental technique is The Atonement. The purpose is to give you the conscious experience of being at one with Our Creator and all the rest of the cosmos. Hence, you can pronounce this "At-One-Ment." You accomplish this by focusing on an elementary vibration of the cosmos; that vibration opens up your experience to the reality of "Your Attributes." For that reason, the technique can also be pronounced "A-Tone-Ment."

Before you begin practicing The Atonement, you need to discover your very own Atonement Vibration. Discovering it is a four step procedure. Have the steps clearly in mind before beginning.

First, sit comfortably with your eyes closed after making provision not to be disturbed. That is, put the animals outside, have the children cared for, close the door, turn on the phone answering machine, etc.

Second, after a minute or so, connect your breathing. That means, breathe normally and easily, but leave no space between the "in" and the "out" breaths. Let the breath be like a huge wheel that carries itself, but keep your awareness on that breath.

Third, discontinue the connected breathing after about ten minutes. Instead, focus your attention on the heart region. In a few minutes you will notice some form of vibration. It might be a pulsation in the heart region that is not from the heart beat. It can also be a movement of your body, such as the head nodding, an arm or leg moving back and forth, or even your whole upper body swaying. It can be in the form of a sensation, or a vision, or something you hear. These are all forms of a vibration, a repeating

PART I / The Basic Tools

action. Some form of a vibration will come to you. If it takes several sessions, don't worry. You can take all the time you need until you recognize your own unique Atonement Vibration. However, never spend more than a total of twenty minutes including the connected breathing at any single session.

The fourth step is to lie down a couple of minutes. If you don't, you may feel rough or irritable.

Invest in a journal to keep a running account of your experiences with all these techniques. For the first entry, describe The Atonement Vibration you discover. From time to time the vibration may change. Note those changes in your journal when they occur.

Once you have The Atonement Vibration, you are ready to learn the fundamental technique called The Atonement, which you'll do twice daily for twenty minutes each.

"Twenty minutes, twice a day?!" you no doubt exclaimed. Yes. Twenty minutes in the morning before breakfast. Twenty minutes again before dinner. Each and every day. You must commit yourself to these two sessions. The success of the techniques depend on your commitment. If you aren't willing to make that kind of a commitment to yourself, it is senseless to go into this material. You gain nothing except inspiration if you only read it. Inspiration won't change your denial to belief or deliver an experience of Truth. Only by practicing The Atonement and its variations that follow in the next chapters can you whittle away at the denials you've held for eons. You can easily do it, but you must perfect and practice the techniques. There is no substitute.

22

The Atonement

What would you gain from reading a cookbook? Entertainment? Perhaps some inspiration? Ideas for conversation? But you would not experience the taste of fine cuisine.

It is the same with this book. To eliminate stress and to gain perfect health, you must do the techniques.

The Atonement is in three easy steps.

First, sit comfortably with closed eyes after making provisions not to be disturbed.

Second, allow The Atonement Vibration to appear and keep your attention on it for about twenty minutes. It is okay to have thoughts along with the vibration, just favor your awareness of the vibration. Keep track of time by looking at a clock once in awhile. If you go to sleep, that's fine. The time asleep counts.

Third, stop focusing on The Atonement Vibration a couple of minutes before opening your eyes. This is very important. Don't just get up; that might cause you to feel irritable or rough.

That's it. <u>Discover The Atonement Vibration. Then use it in The Atonement for twenty minutes twice daily. This is the fundamental technique. Everything else in this course builds on it.</u>

PART I / The Basic Tools

DISCOVERING THE ATONEMENT VIBRATION

STEP ONE: After making provisions not to be disturbed, sit comfortably with closed eyes for a minute or so.

STEP TWO: For about ten minutes connect your breathing so there is no space between the "in" and the "out" breaths.

STEP THREE: For another ten minutes focus on your heart region and notice a vibration in the form of a pulsation somewhere, a movement of the body, a vision, a sensation, or something you hear. That is The Atonement Vibration.

STEP FOUR: Lie down a couple of minutes to avoid roughness or irritability. Afterwards, write a description of The Atonement Vibration in your journal; also enter a record of any changes the vibration goes through from time to time.

THE ATONEMENT

STEP ONE: After making provisions not to be disturbed, sit comfortably with closed eyes for a minute or so.

STEP TWO: For twenty minutes allow The Atonement Vibration to be in your awareness, even if along with other thoughts.

STEP THREE: Wait another couple of minutes before opening your eyes after moving off the awareness of The Atonement Vibration. If you come out too quickly, you may feel rough or irritable.

Chapter Four

Claiming All-Knowing Intelligence

One of "Your Attributes" is All-Knowing Intelligence. At first blush this seems pompous to think, let alone say. Perhaps you have a polite modesty that makes it hard to expound, "I am All-Knowing Intelligence."

You probably avoid "know-it-alls," and they certainly are not your role models. Do you take on their pompous air by proclaiming you are All-Knowing Intelligence?

No! It is just the opposite. The more you know about your Self and creation, the more humble you become. To realize your own nature is to marvel Our Creator. Knowledge brings a heightened appreciation for every blade of grass, each of the species, this beautiful planet, the galaxies—indeed, every aspect of creation.

Furthermore, to know your Self is the foundation for knowing the basic nature of everyone else. "Your Attributes" are everyone else's attributes as well. The Truth elevates the status of everyone to the highest level.

Contrast that with the typical "know-it-all." He tries to stand out as better than anyone else. He pretends to know more, and he suggests he alone has the answers. Instead of empowering you to tap into your own All-Knowing Intelligence, the "know-it-all" tells you his

PART I / The Basic Tools

answers. In actuality, that kind of person operates from weakness, feelings of inferiority, and ignorance. This is not a person grounded in All-Knowing Intelligence.

You are created by some force or energy that must be extremely smart. All of creation came from that same source. Our Creator has to be intelligent. Just take your physical body. Such perfection. Each system in it is so perfect, so efficient, and so complicated that the most educated person does not fully understand it. The nervous system alone boggles the imagination with its billions of neurons, with the way the cells communicate, with the delicate balance of chemistry, with its regenerative powers, and with its problem solving capabilities. What intelligence there must be to perceive and design such incredible machinery! What intelligence there must be to pull together all kinds of material to assemble your body! And what intelligence there must be to guide the ongoing replication of your body!

Your body is just a hint of that intelligence. Consider the ingenious design using photosynthesis for plants, or the perfect balance in the earth's ecosystem, weather, movement of continents, and rotation. Consider the makeup of solar systems, or galaxies, or an expanding universe. Or consider the smaller order of molecules, atoms, electrons, quarks, or fields.

You can not escape the perfect order in which you exist. Even seeming chaos is ordered. It is all predicable, simple, and exact. <u>Everything is perfect. Nothing is not perfect. If it seems imperfect or chaotic, it is only because the whole picture is not understood</u>.

Claiming All-Knowing Intelligence

This incredible place and everything around it is made in the image of Our Creator. To know and appreciate the beauty of the world is to know Our Creator. To marvel in the perfection of the smallest cell or the giant heavens is to feel Our Creator. That is why the next technique is so special. It is to become an on-going frame of mind. "Constantly Marvel." That's all there is to do. "Constantly Marvel."

Verbalize it with friends: "Isn't that flower marvelous?" Think it to yourself: "What a marvelous fly; look at that detail." Never let a moment go by without marveling at the beauty, the perfection, the orderliness, the efficiency, the abundance, the variety, the complexity, and the simplicity of your world.

To do so opens your awareness to your connection to all of that. This is one habit which by itself can change your health. That doesn't imply you can to stop here and gain the full value of this course. Just realize how powerful this one simple habit can be.

To marvel at your world is to bow down in reverence to the intelligence that created you. It is to worship Our Creator. As you do so, the love in your heart grows in appreciation for Our Creator. At the same time, the love in your heart grows in appreciation for your own Self because you are made in the image of Our Creator.

To marvel at the world around you is really to marvel at your own Self. Reading these words does not make that come about. Words alone cannot do that. There is nothing you can read that can open up your appreciation of your Self. This must be experienced, and to "Constantly Marvel" is the beginning of that experience.

PART I / The Basic Tools

The intelligence you're marveling is your own intelligence. Remember, to realize this does not make you pompous. You aren't becoming the "know-it-all" you abhor.

The intelligence behind the entire cosmos is your intelligence for your use. The intelligence of Our Creator that designed and constructed all the infinite kinds of plants, animals, elements, compounds, planets, galaxies—indeed every facet of creation—is your intelligence to carry out your cosmic purposes.

However, the intelligence is available only when you are flowing and in tune with your cosmic purposes. Whether you know it or not, you came into this life with certain things to accomplish. Maybe you have some growth, or maybe you are to teach others. They could be most anything except to harm yourself or others.

If harm is involved, you've deviated from your cosmic purposes. Of course, you are free to deviate because you always retain your freewill. However, if you do so, the All-Knowing Intelligence of Our Creator is not available. In that case you are on your own with a limited intellect.

All-Knowing Intelligence is always available for your cosmic purposes without asking for it. It is always there, always has been, and always will be. That is your nature. That is the way you are created. It is one of "Your attributes."

Most people on earth have lost conscious touch with All-Knowing Intelligence. One goal of this course is to bring it back into focus. After all, to gain command of intelligence is necessary if you are to master perfect health and rid yourself of stress.

Claiming All-Knowing Intelligence

Stress, suffering, and illness naturally arise when you lose awareness of your connection to All-Knowing Intelligence. Whatever else you are to accomplish, regaining conscious connection to intelligence is always a top priority in your life. All the forces in nature support and guide you in the quest to open your awareness. That's why you can't fail with these techniques when you have the desire to succeed.

You already have the foundation to access All-Knowing Intelligence. It is The Atonement. Each time you do The Atonement, you strengthen your conscious bond to All-Knowing Intelligence. Quite spontaneously your thoughts become more powerful. Answers to problems come easily. In fact, problems are avoided without your even knowing of imminent pitfalls. The longer you regularly practice The Atonement, the more you become aware of your connection to All-Knowing Intelligence, and the more powerful your thoughts and ideas become.

The next technique adds dimension to your daily practice by giving you "Yes" and "No" Tools. With them you are in a position to get answers of "Yes" or "No" to any question related to your cosmic purposes. This technique makes it easier to differentiate the Truth of All-Knowing Intelligence from the babbling static in your mind.

The procedure to discover the tools is easy. After about ten minutes into The Atonement, think, "Give me the 'Yes' tool." It is a body movement someplace, a feeling, a sensation, or anything else that is pleasant you can easily notice. When the tool appears, practice it for the rest of the session, so you can recognize it every time you ask a question with a "Yes" answer.

PART I / The Basic Tools

At the next session of The Atonement, repeat the procedure to discover the "No" tool. When you have both "Yes" and "No" tools, practice them during the second half of The Atonement for several sessions. Don't ask questions yet. That requires additional instruction.

Write in your journal a description of your "Yes" and "No" tools. From time to time they may change, so leave a space for describing the changes when they occur.

Now, don't fret if these tools don't come the first time you try. You're asking your physical nervous system to do something it has never done before. Some healing or some restructuring may be necessary. Subtle changes take place in your body so you can perceive these tools as well as The Atonement Vibration. In fact, those changes are the first body changes leading to perfect health and freedom from stress.

CONSTANTLY MARVEL

Constantly marvel at the world around you. Voice appreciation for the beauty, the perfection, the orderliness, the efficiency, the abundance, the variety, the complexity, and the simplicity of Our Creator's handiwork.

DISCOVERING "YES" AND "NO" TOOLS

During the second ten minutes of The Atonement, think, "Give me the 'Yes' tool." The tool is a body movement someplace, a feeling or sensation, or anything else that is pleasant. When the tool appears, practice it for the remainder of the session so you can recognize it every time you ask a question with a "Yes" answer.

At another session of The Atonement, repeat for the "No" tool.

Write a description of the tools in your journal.

PART II

LAYING THE FOUNDATION

Chapter Five

Being A Creator

<u>Since you are made in the image of Our Creator, it naturally follows that you are also a creator.</u>

Some people may think it is blasphemy to give yourself the same qualities as Our Creator. It is not blasphemy. <u>Not to accept your true Self with all "Your Attributes" is the real blasphemy.</u> When you deny your worth, you are insulting your maker. <u>To acknowledge, to love, and to loudly exclaim for all to hear what you are is the true worship</u> of Our Creator in the <u>highest manner.</u>

What kind of a creator would make a product inferior to what he or she is capable of? A soppy creator would. A selfish creator would. Our Creator is neither sloppy nor selfish. Our Creator is infinite love and only wants the most and very best for all creation. To think Our Creator could bestow on you less than everything is to think Our Creator is less than love, less than giving, and less than generous. That, dear friends, is the true blasphemy.

Yes, you are a creator. Say that out loud now. "I AM A CREATOR."

This is not something you need to learn. You are made in Our Creator's image. That is done. You aren't made to go through a myriad of

PART II / Laying The Foundation

lessons to gain creator status. You are now, at this moment, already a creator in the same way Our Creator is a creator. You can't change that fact. You might forget or deny it, but you can not ever take away "Your attributes."

And what do you create? You create your world, your own reality, your own experiences. Want to know how you are using your power to create? Just look at your life. That is what you have created.

However you view your own life, it is clear that most people on earth have missed their mark. They've created wholesale suffering, famines, wars, poverty, crime, pollution, stress, and diseases. No person on earth is untouched by the terrible mess.

"If Our Creator is so loving," you might ask, "how can such a frightful situation be allowed to exist on earth?" Our Creator gave humans freewill to create anything. That means anything. It is not monitored. You aren't told you can do this, but not that, like children are told. You are given full free reign to exercise your freewill.

"This is nonsense. I don't want suffering. It isn't my will," you insist. To understand how a world so devoid of love could come about, you have to understand the mechanics of creating.

A thought begins the process. Some religions say God spoke "the word." That is the same as saying God began His/Her creation with a thought. In the same way your thoughts stir the unmanifest and muster all the resources of creation to their beckoning call.

Creating is that simple. Think what you want and presto! That is exactly the way it happens, but it doesn't seem that easy. You believe many experiences come your way you never had

36

thoughts for. The reason is that many of your thoughts are subconscious. Your mind is so well engineered and efficient that your thoughts can be broadcast automatically with no effort by you. They are programmed into your subconscious mind to keep creating without your having to think them consciously each time. Thoughts in the subconscious remain there until you clearly and unequivocally remove them.

Many of your experiences come about because of those subconscious thoughts. <u>If you are ever going to change your experiences, you must also identify the thoughts you automatically think.</u> For instance, at some time you may have believed you could get more love and nourishment if you were frail. The recurring thought is, "I want to be frail so I will be more loved and nourished." That becomes part of your subconscious, and it broadcasts loud and clear until it is removed.

Your subconscious mind is a marvelous device. Since you are constantly molding your world with your thoughts, you need the subconscious. Otherwise you would have the impossible task of constantly thinking consciously every single ingredient for your experiences. There would be no time to simply enjoy. The subconscious is beautiful, and it deserves to be applauded. Besides, it is a part of your design, and it isn't going to go away.

If you want perfect health without stress, you can easily create it because perfect health is natural. Illness is not inevitable. It is not part of the human condition. Our Creator never could have created you with defects so you would suffer. Anything less than perfection is brought about by your own power to create.

PART II / Laying The Foundation

Before you can continue on this path to perfect health, you must take responsibility for what you experience. Accept your role as a creator. Claim your power. You do that by thinking it with belief.

After ten minutes of The Atonement, think, "I am a creator, and I claim my power." Back off the sentence and return to awareness of The Atonement Vibration. After a minute or so impulse the sentence again, and return to the awareness of The Atonement Vibration. Continue in this manner to the end of the session.

These are power packed words, and they aren't to be restricted to The Atonement. Think them often, any time, and any place. Until you believe you have the power to create your experiences, your desires are thwarted from the beginning.

You must also monitor all your conscious thoughts. This is nothing new. Psychologists and stress managers have suggested this for years. Whenever you hear something you don't want, say, "I cancel that." Then replace the thought with what you want.

For instance, it isn't unusual for people to be afraid of getting into an automobile accident. "I'm afraid I'll get rear-ended, this stop and start traffic is so crowded," you might think. In that case say, "I cancel that thought. I am safe and all traffic flows around me safely."

Fear thoughts are particularly troublesome because people create what they fear. After all, those fears are uppermost in their minds, and the thought of the fear can set into motion events leading to the dreaded experience.

Being A Creator

What you think is what you get. The laws of nature operate without judgment. You are the boss. You get what you put into the atmosphere as a thought. All the power of creation is mustered to stir the ethers to manifest your thoughts, and no-one is out there making sure that what you say is what you really want. What you think is what gets delivered without judgment.

The process is simple. It is just a matter of thinking. Begin now to monitor your thoughts, and continue forever. These laws of nature are not going to change, so you always need to be careful of what you think.

Ignorance of these laws is largely responsible for the dilemma people on earth find themselves in. Certainly, ignorance is perpetuating the dilemma. When people realize the power of their thoughts, the world condition will change quickly. For your contribution, always be aware of what you're creating. Monitor your thoughts.

Of course you can only monitor the thoughts you're aware of. The next technique is for coming to grips with thoughts you're not aware of. This technique uses the "Yes" and "No" tools, so be sure you have a clear experience of them. "Correcting Subconscious Thoughts" is a three step process.

First, begin with ten minutes of The Atonement.

Second, after the ten minutes think, "What is an untrue subconscious thought I have that causes stress or interferes with perfect health?" Listen for the answer. It comes as an ordinary thought. When you have it, ask if the thought about so and so is an untrue thought that causes stress or interferes with your perfect

PART II / Laying The Foundation

health. Use your "Yes" and "No" tools to get the answer.

Third, think, "Give me the correct thought to replace that untrue thought in my subconscious." Again, the correct thought comes to you as an ordinary thought, and verify it with your "Yes" and "No" tools. It is also important that you feel your intention to correct the untrue thought. *Intention* is the reprogramming agent.

When you have identified the untrue thought and the correct thought, write them both in your journal, clearly labeling each. Then repeat the second and third steps to fill out the twenty minute session. Do this in as many sessions as you need to identify all the subconscious thoughts you need to correct.

These three techniques lay a solid cornerstone for your perfect health. Begin now to claim your power—and never let up. Begin now to monitor your thoughts—and never let up. Begin now to correct your subconscious thoughts—and never let up.

ENLIVENING YOUR POWER

After ten minutes of The Atonement, think, "I am a creator, and I claim my power." Back off the sentence and return to The Atonement Vibration. After a minute impulse the sentence again, then back off. Continue in like manner to the end of the session.

You may think these power packed words any time and any place. Think them often.

Being A Creator

MONITORING THOUGHTS

Keep in the back of your mind an active monitor that looks out for conscious thoughts you do not want manifested. When one creeps in, think, "I cancel that." Then replace the thought with what you want to create instead.

Write in your journal the thoughts that recur, and follow your progress in turning them around.

CORRECTING SUBCONSCIOUS THOUGHTS

STEP ONE: Ten minutes of The Atonement.

STEP TWO: Think, "What is an untrue subconscious thought I have that causes stress or interferes with perfect health?" Listen for the answer as an ordinary thought, and verify the answer with your "Yes" and "No" tools.

STEP THREE: Think, "Give me the correct thought to replace that untrue thought in my subconscious." Listen for the answer as an ordinary thought, and verify it with your "Yes" and "No" tools. Feel your intention to change the untrue thought with Truth.

STEP FOUR: Repeat Step Two and Step Three to complete the twenty minute session.

STEP FIVE: Write in your journal both the untrue and correct thoughts you discover, clearly labeling each.

CHAPTER SIX

Common Consciousness

By now you can see the interconnection of these techniques. They intertwine for maximum results. The more comfortable you become with The Atonement, the more natural will be your "Yes" and "No" Tools. That in turn opens up confidence for discovering your subconscious programming. The more that program is changed, the more perfectly all your organs and body systems function. A perfect body is the foundation for experiencing "Your Attributes," and realizing them leads to being even more comfortable with The Atonement. And so the cycle goes.

Every technique you learn is interdependent and interconnected with all the others. You will rarely do just one. Rather, your daily sessions will combine several techniques. During this course, you are told the combination to use. However, after you've mastered all the techniques, you will compose the variations. The needs of the day and the problems you're confronting will lead you to the perfect choices. It is a mix and match game that keeps the procedure from becoming routine, rigid, or boring.

For instance, you may have already discovered one of the best times to think "Your Attributes"

Common Consciousness

is right after you close your eyes for The Atonement. This induces relaxation and peacefulness so The Atonement Vibration can appear more quickly and clearly.

Besides your own thoughts that are more or less personal to you, there are ideas, rules, and beliefs that people share called Common Consciousness. It can be held by a family, a group of peers, a town or region, a country, the West or the East, or even by humans everywhere. They are held both consciously and subconsciously.

This phenomenon is good. In fact, it is part of the grand scheme of creation. A problem arises, however, when there are ideas, rules, and beliefs that hide knowledge of who you are. Social beliefs that deny "Your Attributes" destroy the basic fabric for a quality life.

For instance, today there are social beliefs that suffering is to be expected, that life is a struggle, and that illness is inevitable. Once you buy into those beliefs, they become your own thoughts and the basis for your own experiences. Remember, you are a creator, and whatever you experience begins with a thought. Often the thoughts that you use have their origin in Common Consciousness.

How can this come about? How can thoughts someone else holds influence you? It seems akin to an outside force which you have started to accept as impossible because you are wholly responsible for your own experiences.

Common Consciousness is really proof of how perfect the universe is. The laws of nature are incredibly efficient. Not a single ounce of energy is ever wasted, and the phenomenon of Common Consciousness demonstrates that efficiency.

PART II / Laying The Foundation

When you came into this life, you had countless things to learn so you could function in your society. Instead of teaching you all the ideas, rules, and beliefs the society holds, you are given immediate and constant access to them. You have your own on-board computer storing everything your society thinks. This is a most efficient way to impart knowledge. It is not unlike instinct in animals.

Your mind constantly searches Common Consciousness for relevant ideas, rules, and beliefs. You are free to accept or reject them. Most people are passive in the process and subconsciously accept most of them without question. This works fine, as long as the culture passes on Truth. Unfortunately, Truth is often interlaced with superstition, falsehoods, prejudice, and error.

Common Consciousness could be the source of immense power for everyone. It could impart knowledge about your divine worth—that you are literally created in the image of Our Creator. It could alert you about the role of your own thoughts in what you create. It could expose for you the nature of time or timelessness and the time-space-matter relationship. It could teach you the laws about love and what forgiveness really is. It could guide you to perfect health, the natural flow of wealth, and infinite energy. In essence, Common Consciousness could empower. It could literally enlighten.

Eons ago humans on earth lost sight of their own nature. They denied they are made in the image of Our Creator, instead opting to feel vulnerable, weak, and inferior. They forgot their connection to all of creation and how they fit into the time-space-matter relationship. They

Common Consciousness

distorted love and its simple role in life. As a consequence they brought suffering, illness, and poverty into their lives.

What a shame!! Humankind is royalty, wallowing in the abundance and the perfection that nature attests to. Yet, this royalty opts to ignore their status. In nearly every culture of this world, that is the condition of its Common Consciousness. No wonder so many citizens go into crime. No wonder they're destroying nature with pollution and plunder. No wonder people are miserable.

"No wonder." That says it all. The world and everyone in it is a wonder beyond description. Wonder filled. Wonderful. But with the Common Consciousness of today's societies, the wonder is obscured. People perceive "no wonder."

All the great religious of the world have stories about falling from grace, like Adam and Eve. These stories simply tell of the sad time when humankind opted to deny "Their Attributes." That is where most people are today. It is so sad.

In spite of the condition of Common Consciousness, nothing has changed in Truth. Each person is still exactly as he or she is created. That can never change. The perfection is always present. However, a distorted Common Consciousness does distort your experiences.

Buy into a Common Consciousness belief that illness is a natural condition, and that is what you experience. The suffering is so real, no words could convince you of your underlying perfection. In fact, you are even more convinced the Common Consciousness belief is correct. The whole damned cycle is self perpetuating. And a damned cycle it is—damned for a life of hell on earth.

PART II / Laying The Foundation

It might seem that nature is flawed to allow such a situation to develop. To the contrary, it actually shows Our Creator's dogged determination to let people create without restrictions. Everyone can create whatever he or she wants, even collectively. If folks want suffering, nothing interferes with their freewill to suffer.

Your task is twofold. You need to change the erroneous beliefs you've bought into. You must also help change false beliefs held in the Common Consciousness of your society. You can help because of your connection to everyone and everything else. After all, it is that connection which makes it possible for everyone to share so many false notions and to lose sight of reality.

Each person that changes his or her own beliefs to be in tune with Truth has an effect on Common Consciousness. Furthermore, the power of Truth is so much greater than untruth, a small group of pure thinkers can literally change the world. They don't need to preach, or write, or in any way infringe on anyone else. They simply need to think the Truth. It takes but a ray of light to dispel darkness.

Throughout nature, order is more powerful than disorder. Take light, as an example. Scattered light waves of an ordinary light bulb dissipate in a few miles. Yet the perfectly ordered waves of a laser light can go to the moon and back with little loss of energy.

Nature constantly tries to bring about more order. Whatever is done to her, she constantly corrects it. All the negative influences on earth can not win against the powerful forces of nature that rectify order.

So, you don't have to change the minds of everyone in your culture to help return order to

Common Consciousness

Common Consciousness, provided you are indeed dealing with Truth. A few people thinking Truth is all it takes. They create rumblings that give rise to social debates and reexamination. On earth right now this is going on. Many time-honored beliefs are up for reappraisal. Some even shift without a whimper.

You do indeed have a meaningful role in transforming beliefs of your whole society. The power of Truth is so strong that it takes a very few people thinking Truth to correct beliefs held in Common Consciousness. After the shift, some people will continue to cling to old false beliefs, but many more will experience "Ah-ha" breakthroughs.

Correcting both Common Consciousness and your own beliefs is accomplished in one stroke with the same technique. You isolate an erroneous social belief you've bought into. Then you correct your belief. By doing that, Common Consciousness is forever altered to some degree, and you leave a powerful mark on the human condition.

This is done with a variation of The Atonement. After about ten minutes into the session, think, "What is a false idea, rule, or belief about health held in Common Consciousness that I have bought into?" The answer comes in your thoughts. Use your "Yes" and "No" tools to verify what you receive is correct. Then ask, "What is the Truth about health to replace that idea, rule, or belief?" When the answer comes in your thoughts, again verify with your "Yes" and "No" tools. Continue in like manner for about another ten minutes. Do this for several sessions until you feel you've uncovered the false social beliefs about health you hold.

PART II / Laying The Foundation

It is also important to feel your intention to replace the false idea, rule, or belief with Truth. *Intention* is the key that unlocks your subconscious and impacts Common Consciousness.

Write in your journal all the beliefs, ideas, and rules that come to you. Include the untrue beliefs as well as the Truth, but clearly label each.

Even though you move on to the next chapters, return to this technique periodically. By doing so, your role for improving life on earth becomes far more significant than you can imagine. You may, of course, examine beliefs in other subjects once you've uncovered the erroneous beliefs restricting perfect health and freedom from stress.

CORRECTING COMMON CONSCIOUSNESS

STEP ONE: Ten minutes of The Atonement.

STEP TWO: Think, "What is a false idea, rule, or belief about health held in Common Consciousness that I have bought into?" Listen for the answer as an ordinary thought. Verify the answer with the "Yes" and "No" tools.

STEP THREE: Think, "What is the Truth about health to replace that idea, rule, or belief?" Listen for the answer in your thoughts, and verify it using your "Yes" and "No" tools. Feel your intention to replace the false idea, rule, or belief with Truth.

STEP FOUR: Write in your journal both the untrue beliefs and Truth that come to you, labeling each.

Chapter Seven

Coming To Grips With Fear

Delving into the subconscious to look at the beliefs underlying your experiences opens up pandora's box. Some of the beliefs stored there are truly beautiful and supportive of all you hope for. Some are twisted distortions. Some you made up and put there. Some reflect Common Consciousness of your culture. All of them are very significant in your life because all have the power to manifest their content!

Because the subconscious is obscured, you may have thought of it as a dark, sinister force. You may even expect ugly memories of the past to raise their heads and ruin the day.

Yes, ugly memories are there, but memories alone have little impact. The real power is in your beliefs. They manifest your experience. The memory of a past event does not carry such force.

When you discover and correct underlying beliefs, the problem is licked. Your memories of them remain, but memories without belief are impotent. You might even be amused that you ever believed them.

Because so much attention has been given to trauma arising from the subconscious mind, it has received a bad rap. Properly programmed, the subconscious is one of your greatest allies.

PART II / Laying The Foundation

As a silent partner, it goes about its work unnoticed and unannounced. It musters resources and energy, and it presents your world to you with little effort. This is its natural role. This it has never stopped doing. Its operation is well and running perfectly. If anything, only your instructions to it need to be modified.

Not everyone needs to change beliefs held in the subconscious mind. Many people on earth illustrate how life is lived with a perfect subconscious program. They live wholeness, enlightenment, and self-actualization. The great religions of the world were founded by such people. Mind you, those people only wanted to show and teach human potential. Unfortunately, their simple messages were lost when huge government-like religions emerged.

How did that happen time and time again? How could the loving example of these enlightened beings be missed? Their messages got distorted because Common Consciousness with false beliefs dominated most people's thoughts. The only way such polluted minds could accept the "messenger" was to make him a deity—a status they held far above their own. Such a shame!

Have you noticed how your life has changed just because of the last few techniques? To discover errors in your beliefs and to correct them ushers in a feeling of power, peace, and happiness. As if on a coattail, all "Your Attributes" hitch a ride with each Truth you uncover.

False beliefs pull down your health. They not only manifest their content, but they are the source of stress. Understanding the role of stress on health is a twentieth century gift. Realizing

Coming To Grips With Fear

the role of thoughts and beliefs on stress is the twenty-first century gift.

In your lifetime, you are witnessing how Truth gradually reestablishes itself in Common Consciousness. For instance, take homosexuality. In 1900 it was considered evil. Anyone with that orientation was sick at best, but more likely immoral, disgusting, and degenerate. If the trait were publicly known, the person couldn't teach in the schools, be in the military, rise up in business, or even socialize in most circles. How stressful that must have been! You can only imagine the role it played on the health of many gay men and lesbians.

The last hundred years has brought changes in Common Consciousness about homosexuality. Some people still cling to the model that homosexuals are evil aberrations of the devil, but many more people have gained insight into the Truth of the nature of homosexuality. Their insight has come about largely because of Common Consciousness.

When both gay and non gay people questioned old moral codes, they brought about dramatic shifts in Common Consciousness. A new option crept in: "The universe is an expression of uniqueness and diversity; homosexuality is just one such expression."

The process of changing social thought accelerated when millions of gay men and lesbians around the world came to grips with who they are and garnered self-esteem. Gay activists also contributed to the change in Common Consciousness by marching, holding rallies, lobbying for laws, and organizing support groups. That led many more people to reexamine their own hang-ups and adopt new beliefs about

PART II / Laying The Foundation

sexuality. Each person's new belief left its imprint in Common Consciousness and influenced everyone else's thinking. The process builds on itself.

Social belief upon social belief has been corrected in this manner. Another example is reincarnation. That is a word only a handful knew one hundred years ago. Even half way through the twentieth century, the concept was foreign to most. Then many people started to explore ancient teachings. They searched for a Truth that exists for all people and for all time.

As a result new beliefs about time surfaced. The explorers discovered that time does not exist as they had thought. They learned time is a function of speed and movement and is not exact measurement. They extrapolated that their life couldn't begin in time, nor end at another time. Instead their life exists with time for all time. The bottom line became obvious: life doesn't begin with a time and end with a time—that is, begin with birth or end with death.

People who incorporate reincarnation into their belief system correct Common Consciousness to some degree. An ounce of Truth dispels a ton of false beliefs. Large numbers of people accept the concept without even knowing why.

Gone are the worries "there isn't enough time" and "I may burn in hell for eternity." What a relief to shed these stress-inducing thoughts!

Everyone's health is impacted when Common Consciousness is cleaned up. This is such a marvelous realization. You do improve the health of everyone while you lay the foundation for your own. It is a true win-win situation.

Fear permeates everyone's subconscious because it is a human reaction that can have a

Coming To Grips With Fear

valuable purpose. When you seek safety, fear is often your guide. Encounter a rattle snake or a lion, and the fear impulse arises. Fight or flee. When you are in danger, fear gives you the message.

The problem with fear comes when it is based on an illusion. Amusement parks have rides that take you on lightning fast bobsleds, or trips to other star systems, or runaway trains. These rides can be frightening, but you know the truth. It is all an illusion, and your seat goes nowhere.

It is the same with life. If you are seeing an illusion and you don't know it is an illusion, you could really get scared. That is the case most of the time you are afraid. You just don't have the facts straight.

Hardly anything is more debilitating on your health than fear, whether or not it is based in illusion or reality. The longer it lasts the harder it is on your body. Fear extracts such a huge toll, you dare not allow it unless it has a mighty good purpose.

Coming to grips with fear can't be done by simply thinking, "Don't be afraid." If you don't know you are on a fake runaway train in the amusement park, no words could calm you. In your mind you are in jeopardy. The only way you wouldn't be afraid is to realize the illusion. When you do, the experience is the same, except you aren't afraid.

Frightful illusions are sprinkled throughout Common Consciousness: the fear of death; the fear of growing older; the fear of going broke; the fear of sex; the fear of being left alone; the fear of not having enough time; or the fear of God, heaven forbid. To rid yourself of such a fear, you need to replace illusion with reality. Of course

PART II / Laying The Foundation

you don't want to get rid of fear that legitimately warns of danger. It could save your life.

The next technique eliminates fear based on illusion. After ten minutes of The Atonement, think, "What is an illusion I hold that makes me feel afraid?" The answer comes in your thoughts. Then think, "What is the reality to replace that illusion?" When the answer comes, verify with your "Yes" and "No" tools. Be sure to intend to substitute reality for illusion. Intention is the key. Repeat several times until the end of the twenty minute session.

Write in your journal the fear related illusions you uncover, as well as the realities to replace them. Label each clearly.

The Truth always comes to you in words you can accept and there are many ways to express the same Truth. For instance, if you discover you are afraid of dying and you expend lots of energy and thought worrying about it, the Truth might come to you in this form: "Life is a continuation with no end, only change. Death and birth are synonyms. When you are born here, you die someplace else. When you die here the change represents a birth somewhere else."

The same Truth might come to you in words you could more easily accept: "God loves you and gave you everlasting life." Never judge what your friend hears as Truth just because the same Truth comes to you differently. Truth is heard differently by different people. The same Truth can be expressed in many forms.

Do this technique for several sessions before moving on. Even then, revisit it periodically to uncover deeper levels of fear related illusion.

You never want fear unless it is serving its legitimate purpose. It might be the one factor standing in your way of perfect health. Discovering and correcting the beliefs underlying groundless fear is a magnificent gift to your body.

REDUCING FEAR

STEP ONE: Ten minutes of The Atonement.

STEP TWO: Think, "What is an illusion I hold that makes me feel afraid?" Listen for the answer as an ordinary thought. Verify your answer with the "Yes" and "No" tools.

STEP THREE: Think, "What is the reality to replace that illusion?" Listen for the answer and verify it with your "Yes" and "No" tools. Feel your intention to change the illusion with reality.

STEP FOUR: Repeat Step Two and Step Three for about another ten minutes.

STEP FIVE: Write in your journal the fear related illusions you uncovered, as well as the Truth to replace them. Label each clearly.

CHAPTER EIGHT

Tapping All-Knowing Intelligence

Fear is of two types: the fleeting fear and the permeating fear.

The fleeting fear arises when you are confronted with a situation, and it disappears when the feared object is removed. Being afraid of someone of another race, or being afraid of heights, or being afraid of snakes are examples of fleeting fears. In each case the fear is probably unfounded. Chances are, the person of another race is friendly; chances are you are safe and won't fall; and chances are the snake is not poisonous.

However, the snake might be poised to strike, or you might be close to falling, or the person might be thinking of attacking you. There may indeed be good reason to feel fear. It can't always be ignored. Perhaps you do need to fight or flee.

The permeating fears are concerned with future conditions and situations, like fearing you might run out of money, or fearing you might get cancer or AIDS, or fearing your spouse might leave you. These fears weigh heavily on your shoulders. People with permeating fears often walk like they're carrying a sack of flour. Every organ and cell in their body feels the burden.

Most of these permeating fears are also illusions without any basis in fact. However, if

Tapping All-Knowing Intelligence

you are out of work and need a job, the fear of running out of money can give the impetus to pound the streets. You might be at risk for AIDS, and the fear can force a change in your sexual practices. If your marriage is on the brink of ending, fear can drive you to a counsellor.

Both types of fear can have a legitimate place in your life. When fear properly warns you of real imminent danger, and when fear directs the proper course of action, then fear is your mighty ally. But when fear is based on imagination and illusion, it places unnecessary strain on every part of your body.

If only you could automatically tell the difference between real and imagined situations, you could improve your health a thousand fold. Well, you can. You are created with an inner guidance system that knows the difference.

Most people seem to have turned off their guidance system. This is like an airline pilot turning off his plane's electronics. Without the equipment the pilot can only use his limited knowledge to guess how to direct his plane to its destination. With the gear the mark is easily and effortlessly reached. No pilot in his right mind would ever turn off such a valuable aid, but that is precisely what so many people have done.

People are flying blind through life. Blind, and deaf, and numb! It is no wonder lives are full of so much stress!

Being made in the image of Our Creator, you are perfect and you are All-Knowing Intelligence. *Perfect and All-Knowing.* Those are two of "Your Attributes." They mean exactly what the words imply. There are neither exceptions nor qualifications. Already, now, in this moment,

PART II / Laying The Foundation

you are perfect, and you have access to all the knowledge in the universe.

This is not a pompous idea. To be pompous is to feel better than anyone else. To the contrary, these Truths elevate you and everyone else. No-one is better because everyone is best.

Doesn't that evoke a good feeling about creation? It is a friendly place. Love permeates everything. There is no judgment of better because everything is created best. Our Creator is so loving, it could not be otherwise. True love would not permit someone or something to be created with less than possible. To end up with less would lead to suffering and a feeling of lack. You are not created to experience suffering or scarcity. Our Creator could not even entertain that as an option.

Then why is there suffering? Why is there poverty? What is wrong? Guidance systems are turned off. People deny their All Knowing-Intelligence. They refuse to see their connection to the universe. Instead they flounder on their own with only the intelligence they could garner in this life. No wonder they feel frightened and alone!

When the pilot turns off his guidance system and tries to fly alone, he doesn't alter basic facts. He still has the system, and he can turn it back on. The plane came equipped with it. The pilot only has to decide to use it. However, the longer he flies without it, the more he forgets it is there. Eventually, he'll even forget how to to turn it back on. Sounds insane, but he might even argue that it isn't there to turn on.

That is the plight of most of the people on this planet. Their guidance systems are not on, and they don't know how to turn them back on.

Tapping All-Knowing Intelligence

Many don't even realize they have a system they're not using.

You marvel at a dog's intuition—actually, the intuition of all animals. It is called instinct, and dogs knows when there is danger. They quickly evaluate all the people and animals they encounter and sense immediately any problems. They respond lovingly to some, while snarling at others. These creatures are tuned in. Their guidance systems are on. They are given all they need for their lives and they are using it. Humans are also equipped with all they need for their lives, but most are not using it.

You can turn on your guidance system by simply turning your attention inward. Instead of focusing on the outer environment, you focus on your own being.

That's all there is to it. Focus on your own being. Now do it.

Great! Done!

What? It wasn't as simple as it sounds?

Actually, it is simple, but the process can't be forced. You can't try. Catching inner intelligence is like catching a piece of lint in the air. Try to grab it, and it eludes you. Yet, when you hold out a wet finger tip, the lint floats to you. This is the role of The Atonement.

Each time you do The Atonement, your awareness turns inward. You tap what resides there, and you bring it back into ordinary waking life. What you tap and what you bring back are "Your Attributes." Each time you do The Atonement, you tap those attributes to enjoy and experience in your life.

At first you get but a glimpse of the attributes. Each time you do The Atonement you get a bigger glimpse. Furthermore, the more times you

PART II / Laying The Foundation

do the twenty minute sessions, the longer you'll feel "Your Attributes" back in activity. This is why a twice daily practice must be maintained. The results are cumulative.

Eventually the glimpse becomes a wide angle view, and all of "Your Attributes" are permanently etched back into your life. This does take time, so be patient. Just keep up the practice with regularity. This is the switch to enliven your guidance system.

With regular practice, you notice that you worry less. Your fears are diminished. This comes about naturally without any thought or effort on your part. When the pilot of the airplane turns on his guidance system, the plane goes smoothly to his destination without worry or fear. Likewise, when you turn on your guidance system, you quickly solve all problems and accomplish all your goals with less effort and thought.

Regular practice of The Atonement connects you to the All-Knowing Intelligence of creation. Everything you do is with full knowledge. Your decisions are so wise you seem to weigh all relevant facts, figures, angles, and options. In fact, you do just that, although it isn't done consciously. The pilot of the airplane doesn't have to know all the data the plane's guidance system analyzes; he just knows the wisest answer is always given. That is also your assurance when you tap All-Knowing Intelligence.

At the most refined level of creation everyone is connected. Everyone shares the most basic, most elementary, and indivisible energy that underlies creation. Because of that link, your own guidance system can read every aspect of

Tapping All-Knowing Intelligence

your environment. It knows when there is something to fear. It can differentiate between the illusion and reality.

The result is no less than astonishing. Whenever you feel fear, you can know it comes as a serious warning of danger. Furthermore, it comes armed with a solution and appropriate action to divert disaster.

That is efficiency in action. Gone are wasted energy and needless stress from fear and worry.

Keeping this in mind, go back over the previous chapters. If you haven't already done so, develop a daily habit of two twenty minute sessions of The Atonement. Use the second ten minutes to reduce fear, to correct Common Consciousness, to change your subconscious thoughts, and to enliven your power. Remember also to develop an awareness of "Your Attributes" by thinking them frequently, perhaps as a prelude to The Atonement. Constantly Marvel at the world around you. Continue to monitor your thoughts, canceling those you don't want to manifest.

The Atonement is the cornerstone for perfect health. Each session lays another stone. Before long you have a solid foundation. It doesn't happen over night. But happen it must. It is just a matter of time.

Chapter Nine

Anger Meltdown

You are much more complicated, and more extensive, and more complete, and more beautiful than you can possibly imagine. Your earthly senses only reveal the tip of your being and dwell mostly on your physical body. They reveal little about your energy/light body which survives in tact after so-called death. That body is quite specific, having a form unique to you.

You don't end there. Layer upon layer, you unfold. As your existence expands you start to share energy and form with others—your immediate soul family, larger cultural groups, the human race, and on and on. Eventually, your body embraces literally everything in creation.

As you look out at the evening sky, you are looking out at your Self. That is your body in its fullest, most glorious state. That is also everyone else's body. It is also the body of Our Creator. Nothing that is Our Creator has been withheld from you. You were given it all—not just to use, but to be.

Expansion of your awareness to include your wholeness is your goal in life. It is not too ambitious. After all, you are already that. There is nothing to modify. There is nothing to learn.

Anger Meltdown

You are already created in the image of Our Creator.

You simply need a slight shift in focus. You've stared at the physical so long it looks like that is all there is. If you stare at anything long enough, it becomes so etched in your mind that everything around it gets blurred or blotted out. You must open up to your Self beyond the physical to encompass the whole picture. You must become aware of your whole body and how you share that body with Our Creator and everything else.

Recognizing your oneness doesn't end your uniqueness. You don't melt into oblivion because you never lose the aspect of you that is unique and individual. You as a personality never disappear.

Neither does becoming aware of wholeness rob you of a special life. You still play and create in time—the here and now. Life continues to be fun.

You can even stay on earth to wallow in the infinite expressions of creative intelligence. This is not a place or a state you are trying to evolve out of. This beautiful place is just one example of the infinite playpens of creation.

Granted, this earth is not the nicest place in creation right now, but it is improving. Soon it will be the Garden of Eden again. All it takes is for earth people to broaden their awareness of who they are. Then they'll see what they've been doing to themselves. This is happening, and before long the balance and flow of nature will return.

Even though you encompass far more than you can imagine, your physical body is a very

PART II / Laying The Foundation

important aspect of you. It is intricately involved in the process of waking up to your wholeness.

While you are playing here on earth—and life really is to be like playing—an earth body is required. When you choose to be on another planet or star system, you'll need the local "space suit" for that place. This physical body is necessary, is good, and is perfect. Grasp that. It is wonderful, and it is not something to overcome.

Poor health is really a by-product of "near-sightedness." As soon as you expand your awareness, you become more in tune with all the healing energies of the cosmos. When you restrict your focus, these healing energies are ignored. They're there, but you aren't using them. Expanding your vision to invite healing energies into your life is the goal for these techniques. Then whatever needs to be healed is healed.

The physical body is so much a part of your being that you can't elevate your awareness without improving your health. Likewise, you can't improve your health without expanding your awareness. You know that. It is your experience already. How many of "Your Attributes" do you feel when you're sick? How many when you're in peak health? There is a correlation.

Even The Atonement can be analyzed by how it effects your physiology. After a few minutes into the session, you no doubt notice shallower breathing and relaxation. All your body processes slow down. That slowing down creates rest, and rest accelerates natural healing.

If you prefer, treat The Atonement strictly as a relaxation tool, knowing that rest promotes health. The expansion of your awareness takes place automatically. You don't have to understand how The Atonement works, or even believe that it does.

Because your physical body is important in any path to enlightenment, various physical techniques aid in the quest for wholeness. Hatha Yoga is an age-old example. Also, many people swear that their meditation is their daily jog or a swim. There is no doubt these exercises do expand awareness. They usher in more energy, peace, happiness, and all the other of "Your Attributes."

Because of the role of your physical body, special breathing can also help you in coming to grips with fear and worry. It does not replace cleansing your subconscious mind, but it aids in cutting the guts out of irrational fears.

You've already experienced connected breathing. You used it to get The Atonement Vibration. Simply sit quietly and breathe naturally with no space between the "in" and "out" breaths. Keep your awareness on the breath. An effective variation is to breathe through one nostril at a time, changing nostrils before each exhale.

Interestingly, you can get the same effect with deep and rapid breathing. That is why joggers and swimmers swear their exercise is their meditation. It has a similar effect. Just do whatever physical exercise you do best to get your breath going fast and deep. Everything follows from there.

If you can't exercise, you can get the same results breathing deeply and rapidly. If you begin to feel uncomfortable, lie down. Don't push this one, so as to get dizzy or feel faint.

PART II / Laying The Foundation

Since anger belongs to the same family as fear, these breathing techniques can also help you come to grips with anger. Like fear, anger almost always comes about from narrow vision. When you truly see the whole picture, you are seldom angry. Nevertheless, until your awareness expands, needless anger bubbles up from time to time.

As with fear, anger can be positive. That is, sometimes anger is simply rising to the occasion. Sometimes you must get angry to be effective. Remember the story of Jesus's reaction to the merchants in the temple. The emotion of anger is not necessarily borne from ignorance. It is actually part of your inventory of tools to be used for positive gain. So, the goal is not to obliterate anger and your ability to have it. Your goal is to perceive clearly so you don't get angry without good cause.

If you find yourself getting angry, you need to diffuse it quickly or rise only to the occasion required. This is a volatile, potent emotion, and you do not want to abuse or misuse it. Anger—even when it is needed in rising to an occasion—produces stress with ill effects on your health. Therefore, you only want it when its usefulness outweighs its toll.

The most effective way to neutralize anger and the stress it brings it to administer an antidote. The antidote is love, and you administer love by thinking four sentences made from four powerful words: Love, Heart, Give, and Receive.

Whenever you feel angry with someone, picture the person and think, "I give you my love; I give you my heart; I receive your love; I receive your heart." Focus on your heart, and back off the sentences for a minute or so. Feel

Anger Meltdown

love well up to neutralize the anger. Then repeat a few more times.

If anger is based on an illusion, the feelings quickly dissipate. If you're experiencing anger that is required for the occasion, your reactions are appropriate. That is, your actions solve a dilemma and don't create more problems than they solve. Keep in mind that you can seldom justify hurting anyone or destroying property. Those are usually overreactions stemming from mistake and illusion.

When you use this technique, write in your journal the situation when it is needed and how the four sentences helped manage the anger.

Managing anger is an ongoing challenge. Integrate these techniques into your everyday life to eliminate needless anger. Even when the emotion of anger is necessary, use it sparingly, and then rise only to the point necessary to correct a situation.

The most important anger technique is The Atonement. By practicing it regularly, needless anger fades from your life. When anger is appropriate, you give just the right response. This is yet another incentive to become very good friends with The atonement by twice daily visits.

PART II / Laying The Foundation

BREATHING TECHNIQUES
FOR FEAR AND ANGER

FIRST TECHNIQUE: Sit comfortably and connect your breathing. That is, there is no space between the "in" and the "out" breaths. As a variation, try breathing through one nostril at a time, changing nostrils before each exhale.

SECOND TECHNIQUE: Exercise so as to breathe deeply and rapidly if your health permits. Otherwise sit or lie down and breathe deeply and rapidly.

ANGER MELTDOWN

Picture someone with whom you feel angry and think four sentences: "I give you my love; I give you my heart; I receive your love; I receive your heart."

Focus on your heart and back off the sentences for a minute or so. Feel the love that wells up, neutralizing the anger. Then repeat a few more times.

When you use this technique, write in your journal the situation when it is needed and how the four sentences help manage the anger.

CHAPTER TEN

The Unified Field

What happens when you think, "I give you my love, I give you my heart"? What happens when you say, "I love you" to your sweetheart? Or to your dog? What are you feeling when you fall in love?

To understand love is to understand all of creation. It is to fathom your wholeness. When you feel love you are feeling the common basis of everything.

Albert Einstein theorized about that common basis. He called it The Unified Field. He felt there must be something that everything else is made of—something that unifies everything into one. Science has boiled everything down to space, time, matter, energy, and gravitation. These five are quite different, and they appear to have nothing in common. To suggest that time and gravity are made up of a common field stretches imaginations to the limits.

Of course, Einstein was an exceptional person. He could fathom that all five fundamentals merge into one. He died before he could prove that underlying unity of the universe, but he did take giant steps. To his colleague's amazement he showed that space and time are a continuum. He showed that matter and energy are connected. Scientists are on the verge of proving

PART II / Laying The Foundation

what Einstein knew intuitively: The Unified Field does exist. Perhaps it is proven by the time you read this.

Even more amazing is that you are created to operate from that most refined level. You experience it as love. Love is another word for The Unified Field. You experience the feelings of love when you tap into The Unified Field.

All the great religions recognize this unity. "God is love" appears throughout great immortal teachings. It is the same as saying God is The Unified Field, the basic ingredient that permeates all of creation.

The Unified Field is not made up of billions of units, particles, charges, or bits. It is one single field. It can't be divided. It can't be enlarged. This field is greater than everything in creation, while being smaller than the smallest. Being the simplest, it gives rise to the most complex multifarious forms in creation. Each form has its basis in The Unified Field and can be traced back to it. That includes you.

While you indeed have form and individuality, you ultimately are The Unified Field. That is the point where you share Our Creator's body, and you share it with everyone else. That is what is meant by the expressions "I am that," "Thou art that," and "We are all that." *That* is The Unified Field. *That* is what we all have in common.

That is love. And it is *That* which you feel as love.

Nothing is more powerful than The Unified Field—love. Bring it into your awareness, and you have all of its power. And power it is! This field is single handedly responsible for making, molding, creating, changing, healing, fixing, destroying, and maintaining everything in the

The Unified Field

universe. In the field of physics, it is all three operators: the creator, the destroyer, and the maintainer.

The Unified Field answers to your thoughts by manifesting whatever you think. That is why you need to spend so much time examining and correcting your subconscious thoughts. That is why you must monitor your thinking at all times. With your thoughts—conscious and subconscious—you tickle "that" and stir all the forces in creation to take form. This process is on-going. It never stops, and it has always been your faithful servant. It matters not that your awareness has narrowed and you forgot your connection. The process has never been interrupted.

However, as your awareness expands with the regular sessions of The Atonement, you gain greater conscious control over the process. With full awareness you have the command of The Unified Field that a potter has of his clay.

An example is the spontaneous remission in serious health problems. Quite miraculously, without medical explanation, a person appears to get well. Often this happens almost overnight. Studies have shown that just before spontaneous remissions, patients experience bliss, euphoria, or love.

Do you see what's happening? People who feel a ton of love heal themselves! Somehow, they manage to broaden their awareness. It expands to include their whole immortal Self. With such expansion, they naturally feel The Unified Field. They feel it as love. With awareness focused on love, the desire to be healed manifests.

It is so simple, yet it seems mysterious. Humankind wallows in darkness, trying to fix

PART II / Laying The Foundation

everything on a superficial level. You don't rid your home of termites by addressing only the symptoms. That is, you can't just sweep up their shavings and patch a hole or two. You need to go deep within the walls to tackle the problem.

It is the same with healing. You don't permanently solve your body's physical problems by just addressing the outer shell. Illness is a symptom of a deeper, more fundamental problem. Your ability to tackle it is in direct proportion to the degree in which you have conscious control over the process of manifesting. The greater your control, the greater is your success.

This does not mean you ignore medical treatment for ailments. You need to tackle the problem from all sides. Safety first. Do all that you can. However, if you ignore the natural process of manifestation, you are only patching the problem. It will return, perhaps as a totally different ailment.

The key is The Atonement. Each time you do it, you permanently expand your awareness to some degree. It is like stretching a rubber band. When you let go, the band doesn't quite go back to its original shape. To some degree you permanently expand your awareness at each session. The regular practice cultivates healing love and just may even spark spontaneous remissions.

You don't need full awareness to start healing yourself. The Unified Field is so incredibly powerful that a mere glimpse makes a difference. No doubt you've already experienced feelings of love radiating from The Unified field during the Atonement. This feeling follows you into activity and accelerates healing. In fact, that feeling of

The Unified Field

love may be your real incentive to be regular in the practice.

Expanding your awareness to The Unified field is what heals. The feelings of love arise when the connection is made. From there you manifest your desires for perfect health, freedom from stress, or whatever.

In order to guarantee your true intentions manifest, the ground work to cleanse your subconscious is essential. If you did not do that, begin immediately. You do not want false subconscious thoughts to cloud your experiences. Make sure you are storing in the subconscious what you truly want to manifest. As long as you have an overriding thought or belief, your stated intention may be drowned out and not heard. There's no telling what you'll manifest in its place.

Do you see why those four precious sentences of giving and receiving love are so powerful? When you give your love, you offer the fundamental basis of everything. You offer the attributes of Our Creator because those attributes have their basis in love, The Unified Field. You offer perfection, peace, gentleness, infinite energy, timelessness, every space, abundance, All-Knowing Intelligence, happiness, to mention a few.

And when you fall in love, you are falling into the vat of creation by expanding your awareness. Most people think the feelings of love come from their mate when they're in love. Instead, these are your feelings, feelings that come naturally from greater Self-acceptance and expanded awareness.

The Truth of creation resides in The Unified Field. That Truth is yours to know. It can't be

PART II / Laying The Foundation

otherwise. No wise creator would send his creation into the marketplace without a manual. Your manual is built in. You can access any Truth about the cosmos and the blueprints of the universe directly from The Unified Field. It is all there for the asking. Try it.

After about ten minutes of The Atonement, think, "Let me hear some appropriate Truth about the cosmos." Speak out loud what comes to you in your thoughts. Once in a while ask, "Is what I am saying Truth?" Verify with your "Yes" and "No" tools. If you are incorrect, find out where you erred. Write an account of the Truth in your journal. You can write it out directly as it comes to you, or you can wait until after the session.

Practice feeling love in your heart. Open yourself up to feel it, even for no seeming reason. Just let the feelings of love be present. When you're around people, feel it go to them from your heart region. Do the same for animals, plants, and even objects. Feeling love enlivens The Unified Field, just as enlivening The Unified Field brings feelings of love.

This simple understanding of The Unified Field gives perspective to the cosmos. Everything fits together perfectly, and you are included. Accept your innate connection to The Unified Field and to everything and everyone. The reward is love and Truth. You can't ask for more.

The Unified Field

LEARNING TRUTH

STEP ONE: Ten minutes of *The Atonement.*
STEP TWO: Think, "Let me hear some appropriate Truth about the cosmos." Speak out loud what comes to you in your thoughts.
STEP THREE: Periodically ask, "Is what I am saying Truth?" Verify with your "Yes" and "No" tools. If you are incorrect, find out where you erred.
STEP FOUR: Write the Truth in your journal. You may do it directly as it comes to you, or you can wait until after the session.

FEELING LOVE

Focus on your heart and feel the love that is there, whether or not there is an object for the love. Send that love to the people, animals, plants, and things around you.

CHAPTER ELEVEN

Cultivating Love

To feel love in your life is the ultimate goal. It is the reason you are here now. The earth is going through major transformation, and a renewal of love is its hallmark. Some of the souls on earth now are here as guides and teachers in the process. Others are here to learn.

There are infinite paths that can lead you to enlightenment, and you are drawn to the most appropriate path for either teaching or learning. All paths enliven your awareness of The Unified Field so you can perceive the wholeness of life and experience each of "Your Attributes." Then pure unconditional love is yours. To be aware of The Unified Field is to feel love. Love is feeling The Unified Field.

You experienced how easy it is to focus consciously on love. That simple habit sparks perfection and perfect health. Simply feeling love carries that power because it brings The Unified Field and all it is into your life.

You also bring the feeling of love into your life with The Atonement. With that technique you dip into The Unified Field and automatically get immersed in its feeling—love.

In the state of love, everything is possible. You can literally rearrange atoms. All the powers of nature are at your disposal. That is why

Cultivating Love

spontaneous remissions are not uncommon when there is a sustained period of love. It is the most powerful ingredient in creation. Love is the basis of everything, and everything comes from the one source, love—another name for The Unified Field. It is always at your beckoning call.

Whenever your awareness includes The Unified Field, love is felt. If it isn't felt, your awareness is restricted, and the power of The Unified Field is thwarted.

There is nothing mysterious about these words. Sages throughout the ages have called attention to this power. The great religions were founded on this simple concept, even though complicated doctrines crept in to overshadow the simplicity.

Perfect health carries with it the feelings of love. Conversely, the feelings give rise to perfect health. You can't have one without the other.

The Atonement automatically stabilizes love in your life by expanding your awareness to The Unified Field. With regular and continued practice the feelings become permanent.

Cultivating love is the only worthwhile goal in life. Nothing else matters. It is the only wealth worth accumulating because it is the only wealth you take with you when you leave this planet.

There is no greater gift people give to each other than to give and receive love. Miraculously, just the right people pass through your life to give you a taste of love. It opens floodgates for Self-realization.

Just like the fragrances of flowers are infinite, so is infinite the flavors of love. To experience its many flavors is to experience the many facets of creation.

PART II / Laying The Foundation

You know the nourishment of a mother's love. Or the support of a father's love. Or the approval of a brother's love, the acceptance of a friend's love, the adoration of a spouse's love, and the confidence of a teacher's love. Each love opens different feelings. Yet they are all love, and you know all the feelings as love.

Besides the many flavors of love in its various roles, each person also radiates his or her own particular vibration for love. Think of a friend and feel the love. Think of another friend, and there is a slight shift in the feeling. Yet both feelings are unmistakably love. Like fingerprints the feelings of love each person emits is unique because everyone is a unique expression of The Unified Field.

Your uniqueness will always be. Yet your commonality with everyone will also always be. You are in a sea of diverse beings. At the same time you share a common foundation—The Unified Field. Diversity in unity. Unity in diversity.

The ancients compared unity and diversity with the ocean. The depths of silent water represent The Unified Field. From the silent depths rise each unique wave and ripple. No wave or ripple could exist without the silent depths of the ocean, yet each is unique and separate. Each is also unified with all the others by the silent depths of the ocean.

When a person comes through your life, you experience his or her unique essence of love. Each time this happens, you expand your awareness of The Unified Field a bit more. Each time you rise closer to enlightenment, which is nothing more than the ability to feel love in all its diversity all the time.

Cultivating Love

Love is without condition. It just is. It does not require a reason or even an object. Sometimes this is hard to grasp because it is confused with relationships that do carry obligations and benefits. In a marriage, the parties agree on their roles. Love felt by the parties is independent of those roles. Unconditional love is an overlay to be felt regardless of what is going on in the relationship.

The same is true in business, social, or casual relationships. The parties agree, perhaps by implication, what their duties and benefits are. That is necessary in every kind of relationship. Its success depends on how well each person carries out his or her obligations. Regardless, however, unconditional love can be present. It is not dependent on a relationship, or on how well someone performs obligations. Love is without conditions. It just is. If you lose feelings because a relationship ends, the feelings are not of love. Conditions are foreign to love.

Giving and receiving love is extremely powerful. There is nothing you can't do with love in your heart. You've already learned to quell anger by thinking, "I give you my love; I give you my heart; I receive your love; I receive your heart."

These same four sentences cultivate love. Get into the habit of thinking them in countless situations.

Frequently, throughout your day, look at someone—anyone—and think, "I give you my love; I give you my heart; I receive your love; I receive you heart." Think these sentences for your lover, spouse, and friends. Think the words for strangers on the street. You can't think love

PART II / Laying The Foundation

too often. There is no-one for whom these words are not appropriate.

Just think the words, then back off and wallow in the feelings that rise up in your heart. The feelings are different for each person you think of because your relationship with each person is special and because each person is unique. Some feelings of love may seem more intense than others. Some may appear sexual, while others more cerebral. Some may elicit empathy, and some may even seem indifferent. Yet all feelings are unmistakably love.

Love and attention to and from animals even works wonders. Hospitals and rest homes have discovered that healing is accelerated with animal visits because of love the patient feels. The physical act of petting a cat or being licked by a dog opens up the floodgates of The Unified Field. Try the four sentences on an animal. You will be surprised how it makes you feel. Love is indeed universal.

It is no coincidence that sex is often called "making love." Sex can focus attention on the heart and love. When sex does that, it acts as a path to enlightenment and perfect health. Physical caring and physical contact with other beings is healing and evolutionary. That's why sex is so important to many people.

If sex is natural in your life, let it help enliven love. Feel your partner in your arms and think, "I give you my love; I give you my heart; I receive your love; I receive your heart." Keep these sentences silently with you during the entire love making. The words open your soul to your mate's. It is as if you climb into each other. This expands your awareness to the connection you

Cultivating Love

have to each other. It enlivens The Unified Field you experience as love.

Sometimes you may feel miffed, upset, hurt, or mad at someone. These feelings can be neutralized by thinking of the person along with the same four sentences: "I give you my love; I give you my heart; I receive your love; I receive your heart." Feelings of love displace negative feelings.

As long as negative feelings fester, it is impossible to find solutions. By thinking the four sentences, layers of illusion melt away, and major problems become trifling incidents. When you are in the space of love, you have all the power and knowledge of The Unified Field to resolve any conflict.

Love is the foundation for everything you do in life. Open up to it in every way you know how. The Atonement and its several variations are a beginning. Then develop the habit of giving and receiving love throughout the day in all your encounters and activities. The feelings of love with all its power are bound to surface.

When you have special experiences with these four sentences, write about them in your journal before they vanish like smoke.

Only the most blind and stubborn could miss love. Once it is found, the goal of perfect health and a life free from stress is yours.

PART II / Laying The Foundation

THE LOVE CONNECTION

Frequently visualize someone and think, "I give you my love; I give you my heart; I receive your love; I receive your heart."

Then back off and wallow in the unique feeling of love that comes.

MAKING LOVE

In the act of sex, think, "I give you my love; I give you my heart; I receive your love; I receive your heart."

Feel the love that bubbles up.

THE LOVE MELTDOWN

Whenever you feel irritated with someone, visualize him or her, and think, "I give you my love; I give you my heart; I receive your love; I receive your heart." When the negative feelings subside, work out a solution to the problem you have with the person.

PART III

STRESS MANAGEMENT

Chapter Twelve

Body Consciousness

To understand your body, you need to know the scheme of nature. The body fits right into the pattern, which is both simple and complex.

Nature is made up of several types of layers, and each layer is a form of life. That is, each layer in creation has consciousness because everything comes from The Unified Field. The most elementary characteristic of The Unified Field is consciousness. Absolutely nothing is created without it.

One type of layer in creation is the vibration or frequency layer. At each frequency layer there is life and consciousness which is unique and special. For instance, life at the x-ray frequency is quite different from life at the frequency of gamma rays, or the frequency of light rays, or the layer of any other frequency. Each of these layers presents an entirely different creation, and at each level there is environment and life.

Where you are, right now, there are other levels of life at higher or lower frequencies. They are superimposed over each other, existing at the same time and same place. Some people know how to access these other layers and call it the "spirit world." Since there are countless such layers, most so-called clairvoyants don't know

PART III / Stress Management

which frequency they've accessed or how it fits into the scheme of nature.

This type of layering is vertical. The layers appear at the same place and time, like being stacked on top of each other.

You can also layer creation in terms of time because it is not what it appears to be. To do this, pick a place and then stack all that goes on at that place in terms of time: 10,000 years ago, 1,000 years ago, 100 years ago, 50 years ago, now, tomorrow, 50 years hence, and so forth. This is horizontal layering, and each layer also has life and consciousness. Some people actually experience other time layers, as if they are in a science fiction time machine.

The universe can also be layered physically. It has galaxies comprised of stars and planets which support plants and animals that have organs made of cells put together by atoms. Each component of these physical layers is life and consciousness. The galaxy is life, as is the cell and even the atom.

With all these layers of life and consciousness, the universe appears as a huge cube grid. Life and consciousness appear at each point in the cube. You are on a dot within the cube, a dot that isolates your time, your place, and your vibration.

It is through your physical body that you get locked into a point in the cube. For that reason you may feel confined, and long to escape as an astronaut. Governments spend billions of dollars in outer space exploration to escape, but the most they could hope for is to move to a nearby dot depicting a near time, place, and vibration.

In Truth you don't need to escape because you are created in the image of Our Creator. That

Body Consciousness

means that all Our Creator is, or has, or enjoys is also for you to be, have, and enjoy. Our Creator inhabits the entire cosmos. There is no place Our Creator is not. Yet Our Creator is even more than that.

So it is with you. You inhabit the entire cosmos. There is no place you are not. Yet you are also more than that. In Truth the entire cosmos is your beautiful body—whole and perfect. It has neither disease nor weakness. There is nothing to heal and nothing to improve.

Your more limited physical body exists at this time, place, and vibration, which is twentieth or twenty-first century earth in the vibration of visible light. That earth body is made up of cells and organs that are alive and conscious. Each has a purpose for living and can access all the knowledge it needs to fulfill that purpose.

The many forms of life comprising your physical body are for your use. They can and do respond without question to all the demands you make of them. They can even bring about spontaneous remission, or they can manifest illness.

The remarkable allegiance your physical body has to you shows up in studies of people with multiple personalities. When a person flips from one personality to another, the body also flips. Each personality has its own set of beliefs, and the body responds to those beliefs. For instance, the body can exhibit certain sets of allergies and conditions like diabetes for each personality. The body is servant to each personality, and the body dutifully delivers the experience each personality expects.

Your physical body is like a huge factory. The cells are the workers. The organs are the department heads. You are the boss. Each cell

PART III / Stress Management

and each organ knows its job and receives its instructions from its boss—you.

The life force for your physical body and each of its parts is love. All life depends on the feelings of love. After all, life is ultimately only love—The Unified Field. That is its source, energy, and knowledge. If you want your physical body and all of its parts to be perfectly healthy, they must feel love.

An infusion of love to every cell in your body is automatic when you do The Atonement. You know that happens because you feel it. Each cell and each organ vibrates with love. There is no way illness can manifest when the cells bathe in such love energy. It brings the whole body into harmony with the perfection of natural law.

In the hours that follow The Atonement most of the feelings of love dissipate, so another infusion is necessary. Each time a little love sticks and gradually builds up in each cell.

That's why the twice daily practice is necessary. With each session love is infused, then fades away. Eventually, the fading subsides, and love feelings become permanent. It comes about gradually but as fast as is safe. After all, you're asking your nervous system to alter its functioning which requires changes in its structure and chemistry. The final results are inevitable. It only takes time.

You must also consciously deliver love to your body and each of its parts. The bundle of live, conscious cells and organs that respond to your demands are aware of you, and they know all your intimate thoughts.

So, beware! Watch your thoughts about your body. Like the workers in a factory, your physical body—indeed, each cell—responds to

Body Consciousness

the attitudes of the manager. All the cells and organs know what you think of them. They are sensitive, and they respond in kind. If your body is told it isn't liked or appreciated, it will—well, how would you work for a boss who said he didn't like you? Even some indifference is demoralizing. You must voice your appreciation. That is just good management.

Take your hands and run them all over your body with the intention of transmitting love. Let all the cells feel your love. Talk to them. "I love you." "You're doing a great job." "I'm sorry I loaded you down with that pepperoni pizza, but you digested it beautifully." Banter like that. Feel, talk, and send love. It has its effect. Appreciation and love need to be there always.

Knowing how your body fits into the scheme of the layered creation is important for gaining perfect health. Such knowledge gives perspective for what your body really is and what you really are. Then perfect health and freedom from stress isn't so far-fetched.

BODY MANAGEMENT

Run your hands all over your body, while talking to it. Include such words as "I love you," "I appreciate all you're doing to make my life here meaningful," and "We're having such fun together." Speak like this to your body, knowing it is made of many conscious cells and organs that do hear your thoughts.

CHAPTER THIRTEEN

Communicating With Your Body

You are a manager of a very complex and perfectly designed factory—your physical body. It has millions of cells, each with its own life and consciousness. Your body is aware of being alive, of its environment, and of its purpose. It knows from moment to moment what it is doing.

Every cell in your body is plugged into all the knowledge and intelligence of creation. Each cell automatically zeros in on the special knowledge it needs to do its job perfectly and efficiently. Then it goes about its work as an expert.

That is precisely what you're learning about yourself. You too are plugged into all the knowledge and intelligence of creation. You too can know what you need to fulfill your purpose and do your tasks efficiently.

You also have experienced that you can disavow your connection to All-Knowing Intelligence. You can opt to go alone, using only your intellect with the knowledge it has learned.

Does your rejection of All-Knowing Intelligence effect your body's ability to tap that source? It indeed does. Management practices do effect the work force. You are in charge of the whole body system. It is there to serve you, and it takes direction from you. While no cell can be disconnected from its source of All-Knowing

Managing Your Body

Intelligence, each cell must obey management. Each cell must accept without question what you dish out to it.

That is simply the classic management-worker relationship. The infantry obeys what the general orders, even when individual soldiers know it may mean death or serious injury. Your body obeys your commands, even though they may be stupid, ill-advised, dangerous, and senseless.

When you regain a conscious connection to The Unified Field, your demands on your body change. What you dish out always supports rather than thwarts the cells. Then each cell can more easily access All-Knowing Intelligence. The result is perfect health. When each cell in an organ operates at peak performance, the organ runs perfectly. When all your organs are at top efficiency, you experience perfect health.

You are created to have perfect health. The body has flawless design. It is made with each of the billions of cells having a specific job, and they each know how to do that job. That is perfection incarnate. However, the design assumes you would remain consciously connected to All-Knowing Intelligence so you would give intelligent and life supporting commands. That is a logical assumption. Only a lunatic would throw away such a precious gem. Yet people on earth have done just that. The gem is reclaimed with The Atonement.

Good management also requires good communication. You must be able to talk to your body and to hear its input.

Your body and each of its millions of parts do hear you. That is why it is so important to run your hands all over your body with expressions of love. Your cells and organs are conscious

PART III / Stress Management

beings that respond to love and affection. They've never stopped hearing you. Every thought you have reverberates throughout your entire system.

Communication, however, is a two way street. You must also listen to your body. It speaks, but you may not pay attention. You might even tune it out, like a mother tunes out a child screaming for attention.

If you listened to your body, you'd hear about diet deficiencies and preferences, about exercise needs, about rest requirements, and about environmental concerns. You might even hear some love and devotion. You could hear almost anything from your body, but you have to make a point to listen.

The technique to listen to your body is similar to the techniques you've already learned. It is also as simple, but it may take several sessions to feel comfortable with it. After all, you are expanding your nervous system that may require structural or chemical changes.

After about ten minutes of The Atonement, think, "Give me a Body Signal." Back off that thought and notice some movement or sensation that is different from The Atonement Vibration. It can be anything that is involuntary and pleasant. When you have The Body Signal, verify it with your "Yes" and "No" tools, and write in your journal a description of it.

With The Body Signal firmly established, you can listen to your body. Remember, your body has a consciousness of its own. You are not your body. You just inhabit it. The body is a collection of millions of conscious beings, each with its own life and awareness. The body as a whole has

Managing Your Body

its own consciousness, but it also knows everything about each of its parts.

To hear messages from your body, start with ten minutes of The Atonement. Then back off The Atonement Vibration and substitute The Body Signal. When The Body Signal is firmly in your awareness, speak out your thoughts. Periodically verify with the aid of the "Yes" and "No" tools that you are correctly speaking out the message from your body. Besides narrating, you can also ask questions that require only a yes or no answer.

A narrative from your body might run like this:

"It would be good to have more light exercise. The leg muscles want to run, and the cells like the added oxygen that comes with deeper breathing.

"Fat and fried foods are hard to digest. Try more fresh vegetables or fruit. Also, avoid wheat, except for irresistible desserts.

"Instead of the steam room, try the sauna for about ten minutes. It's easier to sweat, and the outer cells don't get as hot."

And so it can go. Your body might come up with very specific suggestions, such as exercise and diet. Or it might be general statements about your path, wisdom, and a body's role. Just be without judgment. Don't ever try to anticipate. Innocently speak out what's in your thoughts. No relationship is complete without a free exchange. Now you can have a complete and meaningful relationship with your body.

After you've finished, write in your journal what you learned from your body. Set aside several pages so all this material can be

PART III / Stress Management

together. It is good to review it periodically to be reminded of habits you need to cultivate.

This technique is a catalyst. You will eventually reach the point you don't need The Body Signal to listen to your body. You'll know intuitively when your body is speaking, and you'll know how to listen.

As you become more conscious of your connection to The Unified Field because of your daily sessions with The Atonement, your habits and practices change to support better health. Listening to your body refines those habits and practices even more.

Until all your actions are spontaneously correct, there are some common sense guidelines for your body. These fall into three categories of diet, exercise, and attitude.

Consume only the food you believe makes sense. That differs from person to person and from time to time. Meat and potatoes may be perfect for one person, while raw vegetables and fruit are required of another. You need to respect those individual differences. Just because your uncle discovers a wheat free diet works best for him doesn't mean it is best for you or anyone else.

Except under the care of a doctor, avoid any drugs or other substances that alter the normal functioning of your nervous system. It may appear that you're having a mind expanding experience with some recreational drugs. In Truth, they overload your circuit and cause injury. This interferes with everything you do in life, including the predicted results of these techniques.

Give your body exercise, but don't strain or tire yourself. Certainly, follow the advice of your physician and be sensible. The point is to keep your muscles limber and strong, your lungs expanded, and your arteries open. Each body has a different requirement for exercise and lets you know what is best.

Finally, continue to monitor your thinking and attitudes. Nothing has greater bearing on your bodies or your health than your thoughts. When you slip into negativity, change the thought. What you think is up to to you.

That's all there is to it. It can actually be fun managing your body so it is stress free and healthy. Go for it. The reward is to experience all "Your Attributes."

DISCOVERING YOUR BODY SIGNAL

STEP ONE: Ten minutes of The Atonement.
STEP TWO: Think, "Give me a Body Signal." It comes as a movement or sensation that is involuntary and pleasant.
STEP THREE: Verify The Body Signal, using your "Yes" and "No" tools.
STEP FOUR: Write in your journal a description of The Body Signal.

PART III / Stress Management

LISTENING TO YOUR BODY

STEP ONE: Ten minutes of The Atonement.

STEP TWO: Back off The Atonement Vibration and substitute The Body Signal.

STEP THREE: With The Body Signal in your awareness, narrate the message your body has placed in your thoughts. Periodically verify with the aid of the "Yes" and "No" tools that you are correctly speaking out the message from your body.

STEP FOUR: Write in your journal what you learned from your body. Review it periodically to be reminded of the habits you need to cultivate.

Chapter Fourteen

Neutralizing Global Stress

Now that you've experienced listening to your body, a word of caution is in order. Do not abandon modern medicine. The temptation is there to ask your body, "Is the new mole on my thigh malignant?" Don't. When you think you might need traditional medical treatment, go for it.

Remember, everything in creation has its basis in The Unified Field. Everything. That includes doctors, nurses, hospitals, syringes, pills, syrups, tonics, ointments, and so on. There is no reason why these can't contribute to your health.

Leave no stone unturned when it comes to your health. That begins, of course, with The Atonement. It is the foundation for Self-sufficiency and leads to perfect health. That does not mean you can be foolish or reckless. Always do whatever is reasonable and necessary from every angle to maintain your health.

If you break your arm, have it set professionally. If you have a growth, let a doctor see it. If you are running a high fever, don't let nature take its course unassisted. You live in a world that offers help. So, get it, but at the same time cultivate the foundation for perfect health and freedom from stress.

PART III / Stress Management

Some people prefer acupuncture, massage, reiki, or some other kind of Eastern approach. That's fine also. Make no judgment about the various forms of healing. Most have some validity. This is the time for your intellect to explore them and make a recommendation.

Even though most people have given the intellect more of a role in life than it is designed to have, it has nevertheless valuable roles. Deciding when to get medical treatment can be one of them because your intellect's legitimate purpose is to evaluate your present situation, inventory your support, and zero in on what you've learned about life.

The intellect can assess all the factors—your symptoms, treatments available, what others say, what you've read or heard, etc. Then it guides you: wait and see how you feel tomorrow, make a doctors appointment, or go quickly to an emergency hospital.

Even enlightened masters get sick once in awhile here on earth. This is a stressed planet now. Everyone is wallowing in Common Consciousness that is full of errors. If you wallow in a mud puddle, you get dirty, regardless of how aware and enlightened you are. Dirty Common Consciousness is bound to leave its mark on everyone.

Some diseases are a reflection of error-filled Common Consciousness. It can't be helped as long as Common Consciousness is full of stress. That's why The Atonement is so important. It is the most powerful contribution you can make to help clean up the mess. Everyone on earth is influenced positively at each of your sessions because everyone is connected to you. You can't broaden you own awareness of The Unified Field

Neutralizing Global Stress

without broadening everyone else's as well. As your consciousness is raised, so is everyone else's raised. The inevitable result is better health and less stress for all people.

At this stage of human transformation, there is another phenomenon taking place. This is unusual in most of the cosmos, but it is happening here now. That is mopping up negativism accumulated by anger, stress, hatred, and revenge from thousands of years of ignorance, wars, turmoil, and planetary abuse.

Negativism has a physical component. Energy balls form whenever there is anger, and they influence everything around them. Until they are dissipated, they foment conflict. A stupid, seemingly endless cycle results, and the world situation gets worse. Anger creates energy balls that give rise to more conflict which creates more energy balls, and so it goes—on and on.

The problem is so acute that there is danger of destroying all life on this planet. Consequently, help has come from around the cosmos, and the negative energy balls are being dissipated in countless ways. In fact, no stone is left unturned.

You are living through a small window of time when the ignorance of a millennium is being reversed. This is a relatively short window, lasting only a few years into the twenty-first century. Why these windows of time open up periodically, then close, is another one of the mysteries to be solved. It is clear, however, that time is not what it appears. It is actually an ingredient of creation arising from The Unified Field. Time has its own agenda with a unique role in forming conditions, opportunities, and

PART III / Stress Management

situations. Everyone plays in time, but everyone is also outside of time.

Confusing? Of course. You are no doubt so wrapped up in time that you can't fathom it is from The Unified Field, or has its own agenda, or that you exist separate from it. Nevertheless, time does indeed march on, and it brings its own set of opportunities. At this moment, time is providing a short period for reversing the devastating cycle of anger and conflict on earth.

This period is also marked by a time for enlightenment. People can more easily awaken to their connection to The Unified Field. All this is happening. Ignorance is being reversed. Anger and conflict are being neutralized all over the world. Political and economic restructuring is even taking place.

Although the window of time has opened, time does not act. It only sets up the conditions, opportunities, and situations. People must take advantage of the time, and indeed they are.

The whole universe has responded, not unlike The United Nations sending relief to drought stricken areas, storm torn countries, or starving people. Hundreds of thousands of enlightened souls volunteered to come to earth from other star systems to help the transformation.

Some of the enlightened came to be teachers of new thought and a new world order. Some came to be national leaders to kill imagined fears and hatred. Some came to be antennas of cosmic energies that are being focused onto the planet. Some came to take on false beliefs of Common Consciousness, work through them to illuminate Truth, and thereby change everyone's belief system.

Neutralizing Global Stress

Another group of enlightened beings came to this planet for the sole purpose of dissipating stress. One way they do this is to absorb the energy balls into their bodies. They don't realize this is happening because it is necessary for these enlightened beings to forget who they are and where they come from. They don't even have a vision of their purpose.

When these enlightened souls absorb negativism, they get sick. Many get so sick they have to drop their physical bodies. Then they either go home or come back with another body for another round. This is not a fun job, but it must be done. No stone is left unturned to transform this planet during that small window of time.

Certainly, not all people who are sick are enlightened masters with the role of neutralizing negativism. Disease is most commonly the symptom for renouncing your connection to The Unified Field, and the remedy is The Atonement. Each session takes you a step closer to enlightenment. Each step is permanent, and that is progress you retain. If someone is very sick and begins The Atonement, death may still result, but every ounce of expanded awareness, however slight, is forever open.

There are no physical possessions you take with you at death. However, you do take all progress you've made in becoming aware of your connection to The Unified Field—the awareness of love and Truth. So, at any time in life, regardless of disease prognosis, these techniques are invaluable. Each step of progress made in this life is a step of progress you keep.

Earth has more people now than it ever has. Souls who forgot their conscious connection to

PART III / Stress Management

The Unified Field have come from the far reaches of creation to take advantage of this window of time. This is now a great chance to drive a wedge through ignorance. Without doing anything, every person is bound to be influenced by the changes taking place in Common Consciousness. That means an expanded awareness of Truth, and is kept.

Whatever you pick up here during this transformation can only improve your lot. For many of you, however, the goal of full Self-realization will be met.

Chapter Fifteen

Illness And Death

There are two underlying reasons why people get sick: neutralizing global stress and being unaware of their connection to The Unified Field. Because you don't know which is the root cause, you can't learn anything about someone's level of consciousness by observing their health.

When enlightened souls neutralize global stress, bundles of anger-energy are absorbed into physical bodies. This energy is so strong it often destroys the normal functioning of an otherwise perfect body.

This concept may seem quite bizarre. The idea that negative energy lingers around to haunt society is hard to grasp. That this energy is absorbed by a body to be neutralized stretches the imagination. Nevertheless, this is true.

Some enlightened beings come onto this planet specifically for this purpose. Because of their vibration, they can absorb an extraordinary amount of global stress. However, these enlightened beings aren't the only ones who have to deal with it. No-one is untouched by global stress. Everyone on earth feels this mopping up. It is a burden each and every human on earth must shoulder.

And burden it is! There is so much illness around the world that is unavoidable because of

PART III / Stress Management

the global stress. They all seem so senseless, and certainly unrelated to stress. After all, most diseases can be traced to virus or bacteria. However, there is a closer relationship between global stress and microbes than is apparent.

If people could see the whole picture, it would not be painted with tragedy. Instead it would be a picture of hope and vision. This is the time to clean up the planet.

Whenever an illness results from neutralizing global stress, your only choice is to flow with it. The process is automatic, and it is going to do what it has to do. Even if death seems the inevitable outcome of the illness, the process is perfect. After all, birth and death are only illusions.

Life is not created with birth or destroyed with death. "Birth" and "death" are terms that denote change. Which word you use depends on where you're viewing the change. If you're witnessing from a place in time *before* the change, the change seems like the *end* of something—a death. If you're witnessing from a place in time *after* the change, the change seems like the *beginning* of something—a birth. "Birth" and "death" are synonyms. They are terms used in the field of time.

Scientists now know that time is not a definite value. You can't look at creation and lay out a course of events in exact time measurement. That is, you can't locate a moment, then count the years to the present. It may seem quite logical, but it isn't how the universe flows.

Time is related to speed. The faster you go, the slower time is. A person in a spacecraft for a hundred years may only experience and age twenty earth years. This is a fact, yet it is beyond

Illness And Death

easy comprehension. If you travel fast enough, time stops. Or if you stop moving, time reaches infinity. Actually, time stopping and time reaching infinity are the same—now, that's mind boggling.

All of this play with time effects your soul in no way. That is because you are created outside of time, just like you are created outside of space, of matter, of gravity, and of the electromagnetic field. Yes, you are all of that, but you are also more.

At any time you can pop up someplace in creation, take on the local physical body to keep you there, then enjoy. When you're finished with that place, you can drop the local body and pop up someplace else with no loss of time. You need not grab a spaceship and take several light years to get to another star system. You do it at the speed of thought—literally in no time. "In no time" because you are created outside of time.

This is important to grasp for you to hone in on healing: time is not a factor in anything you—the whole you—do. Of course you think it is. You've given time so much power. In fact, you've probably wished you had more time. Well, you have all the time you need, while you really need no time at all.

You think you need time for your evolution. You want to grow, and you think it takes time. You want to heal and come to grips with your issues, and you think it takes time. Well, you are created with no need for time. It isn't a necessary ingredient. Certainly, it has no role in your growth, or healing, or issues.

This is why people can experience spontaneous remission for any disease. It is a common notion that healing takes time, yet your

PART III / Stress Management

soul and body know there is no such requirement. The healing takes place spontaneously. It requires only your conscious connection to The Unified Field. The connection must be *conscious*. The connection is always there. It can't be severed. However, pulling current through the connection requires the power of consciousness.

This is why people speak of conscious-raising techniques and experiences. The more aware you are of your connection to The Unified Field, the higher your consciousness is said to be. The more conscious you are, the more of "Your Attributes" you experience. No wonder that spontaneous remissions occur after feelings of profound love and bliss. Feeling love is the sure sign of higher consciousness—of a more conscious connection with The Unified Field.

It doesn't matter whether an illness is from mopping up global stress or from being unconscious of The Unified Field. From your side the remedy is the same. The first step in healing yourself is to be without judgment. Don't punish yourself for being sick. Examine your beliefs and change them the best you can. After that, let nature take its course, and don't be harsh on yourself.

Second, do everything physical you can. Go to a doctor. Eat properly. Exercise appropriately.

Next, bring The Unified Field to your awareness with The Atonement or any other technique you're drawn to. There are countless paths. It is more important that you be diligent and regular in some practice than to fret over which path is best.

A variation of The Atonement can give added dimension to all aspects of healing. After ten minutes, back off The Atonement Vibration and think, "Give me a Perfect Health Vibration." This can be any movement, feeling, vibration, or pulsation somewhere in the body that is involuntary and pleasant.

After you feel comfortable with The Perfect Health Vibration use it in place of The Atonement Vibration for about five minutes in each session. This puts you into direct contact with the energies of the cosmos that maintain balance and perfect health. It also signals your clear intention to experience perfect health.

When you have a specific illness, place your hand or finger in the region affected while focusing on The Perfect Health Vibration during The Atonement. Healing energy is directed through your hands, and the healing energy and life force needed to make your body healthy floods your injured or sick cells. Healing is accelerated. As you become more and more conscious of The Unified Field, less time is required because the process is outside of time. Eventually, healing becomes spontaneous with your intention.

Document your healing experiences in your journal. Describe the illness, what you did, the results, time for the healing, and any other interesting details.

It is important to keep in mind you do not know the reasons for your illness. It may turn out to be short lived, or it may be long and terminal. These techniques give you the tools you need to handle whatever is in store. If total healing is best, that is what you'll get. If a great cosmic purpose is being played out, the techniques bring a peace of mind to understand and accept what is happening.

PART III / Stress Management

THE PERFECT HEALTH VIBRATION

STEP ONE: Ten minutes of The Atonement.

STEP TWO: Think, "Give me a Perfect Health Vibration." It appears as a vibration, pulsation, or feeling someplace in the body.

STEP THREE: Replace The Atonement Vibration with The Perfect Health Vibration for about five minutes in each session. This procedure puts you in direct contact with the energies of the cosmos that maintain balance and perfect health.

STEP FOUR: Write in your journal a description of The Perfect Health Vibration.

HEALING SPECIFIC ILLNESS

STEP ONE: Ten minutes of The Atonement.

STEP TWO: Substitute The Perfect Health Vibration in place of The Atonement Vibration.

STEP THREE: Place your hand or finger on the affected area of your body. Healing is accelerated by directing healing energy and life force.

STEP FOUR: Log in your journal any illness that you feel is helped with this technique, along with a description of the experience.

PART IV

THE REWARDS

Chapter Sixteen

Wisdom

Perfect health is reaping all the fruit of your connection to The Unified Field. As you strengthen your conscious awareness of the connection, you open gates for wisdom and knowledge to flow in.

The flow is not a flood. Rather it is an oozing that permeates and soaks thoroughly. Without your realizing it, you are wiser. The right decisions pop up without effort and without having to weigh a thousand options. Your intuition is reliable. You trust your gut reactions, even your first impressions.

If you regularly practice The Atonement, you already experience the first signs of this benefit. If you haven't, let this inevitable payoff be an incentive to become regular in the twice daily sessions.

The development of intuitional wisdom does not take the place of your intellect. You still need to keep abreast of the news to be well-informed. You still need to study the manuals for new equipment. You still need training in specialized work skills. This is what the intellect is for. It processes the knowledge that makes the earth at this time a special place. It ties you as a universal soul to this unique time and planet.

PART IV / The Rewards

Wisdom, on the other hand, spans creation and time. To be wise is to know and understand universal laws and principles. You recognize who you are. You grasp the far reaching extent of your influence. You comprehend how creation manifests. You perceive "Your Attributes." You feel your connection to Our Creator and to every other being. You know how to feel love and to experience all the emotions without losing contact with reality. You fathom how your life relates to all life. You understand birth and death. You appreciate the concepts of time and space. You identify with the basis of everything, The Unified Field.

This is wisdom. It doesn't come with age, because you are ageless, timeless. It comes with existence. Nothing exists in this wonderfully perfect universe that is not blessed with wisdom. It comes with the territory.

There is nothing you need to do to get wisdom. You don't have to deserve it. It is part and parcel of you already, at this moment. Furthermore, there is nothing you can do to lose it, although you can opt to ignore it, as so many people have done. Wisdom is as much a part of you as the rays are part of the sun. All the answers you need to know about your Self, your purpose, and your relationship to everything else is already within you. You just need to be consciously connected to The Unified Field.

A sportsman sometimes makes his game more challenging by giving his opponent a handicap. Perhaps he'll give the opponent extra points. Or he might tie his hand behind his back. In some way he plays with less than what he has. It's like playing with less than all his marbles.

Wisdom

Somehow people have opted to do just that. Now the world is full of people playing with half their marbles. They cut themselves off from wisdom.

"How challenging life would be," they must have thought, "if we dove into life with no intuition and no connection to Truth. We'll just use the intellect. Everything we can use in this life must come from what we can possess and learn while we're here. We won't rely on wisdom."

Perhaps that game would be fun for awhile. Any game is fun that forces you to exercise certain skills. However, the game has gone too far. People are engrossed in the handicap, and they're trapped. The result is an endless cycle of life after life after life, trying to break out of the handicap.

The thought of reincarnation can be comforting. At least it means that death isn't the end, and it is a better alternative to either eternal fire or harp music forever. As true as reincarnation is, it isn't necessary the way it is practiced now on earth. Here the cycle of birth and death stems from the trap. People keep returning to find a way out. They're looking for Truth, for wisdom, and in each life they fail.

They fail because they continue to look only to the intellect. They fail because they deny their heritage, their attributes, their power, their divinity, and their connection to The Unified Field.

The trap of *mortal* reincarnation is very confining. The same problems of poverty, illness, unhappiness, and suffering keep resurfacing. Each life is spent looking for a way to be freed.

PART IV / The Rewards

In contrast, freedom is the hallmark of *immortal* reincarnation. You are free to wander from playground to playground in the universe, like a child wanders from ride to ride in a carnival. At each playground, you use all your wisdom and all "Your Attributes." There are no issues to work through and no suffering. That is the way life is intended to be experienced.

Your immersion in a mortal life-death cycle is an illusion. You never lost an ounce of who you really are. Not one ounce! The repeated failure to return to conscious wholeness does not alter you in the slightest. The failure simply perpetuates the illusion that you are frail, suffering, and mortal.

When you break the illusion to experience all "Your Attributes," you realize you are a wise sage with perfect health and freedom from stress. When you are healthy, you experience all that you are, and that includes wisdom.

While you are locked into this time and space with your physical body, most of your perceptions and experiences come to you from your physical nervous system. However, the physical body and its nervous system mirror the handicap. That means your physical nervous system is not complete. It lacks the circuit for wisdom—for tapping All-Knowing Intelligence.

That is not the way Our Creator designed the physical human body. It is how you modified it. The incomplete nervous system is now the norm for this planet. And a sad norm it is!

The physical nervous system of a person consciously connected to The Unified Field is different. Its structure and chemistry support perceptions, experiences, and knowledge unknown to the unenlightened.

Wisdom

Some universities are studying the physiology of people having experiences associated with higher states of consciousness. Subtle but significant differences in brain waves, blood chemistry, and brain fluids are found.

Each session of The Atonement brings about lasting changes. One reason is because of the deep rest the practice induces. At each session, you settle down and get very relaxed. It is in deep relaxation that the body heals most efficiently. You know that. Rest is always the first prescription for any illness.

A physical body that doesn't match the cosmic blueprint for a physical human body needs "healing." That is, some corrections must be made to bring it in line with the blueprint designed by Our Creator. Restructuring begins at the first session and continues until the nervous system fully supports a conscious connection to All-Knowing Intelligence.

In the same way, other abnormalities are nibbled away. Allergies clear up. Headaches wane. Digestion improves. And so on. Relaxation by itself helps to heal illness, but it is the restructuring of your nervous system that really changes your health. When your nervous system can support a conscious awareness of The Unified Field, true health is an automatic by-product. Then the illusion of mortality, suffering, and frailty is perceived for what it is.

Although wisdom returns to you automatically by just doing The Atonement, you need to practice accessing All-Knowing Intelligence. If you have a new hand blender that grinds coffee, crushes ice, chops nuts, slices cheese, and scrambles eggs, you have to incorporate it into your life. It could sit on the kitchen counter

PART IV / The Rewards

while you hand chopped nuts, hit the ice with a hammer, and scrambled eggs with a fork. You must get into the habit of using the blender, or it will just sit on the counter.

It is the same with wisdom. Although wiser decisions automatically creep into your life, you can multiply wisdom's value by seeking its input and acting on it. That takes practice.

Before starting The Atonement, pick out some situation that needs a resolution in your life. This can be a problem that needs solving, or it can simply be an area you need guidance on. Then after about ten minutes into The Atonement, think, "What is the highest wisdom for me to know about so and so?" Listen for the answer. It comes in your thoughts. At first it is easier to speak the answer out loud, but when you're comfortable with the procedure, you can say it silently. After you've spoken a few lines, verify that it is Truth with your "Yes" and "No" tools.

This wisdom can come to you on any subject. However, it never addresses the future or the past. Only the present has any relevance for wisdom. That's important to always keep in mind. Only ask about highest wisdom for the present.

Set aside a few pages in your journal to write the wisdom that comes to you. Review it once in awhile. If something seems out of date, ask about it again. Generally, however, it is best not to keep asking the same question over and over. That implies you don't believe the answer and aren't relying on it.

Practicing wisdom paves your conscious connection to The Unified Field. Accessing wisdom leads you to perfect health, since

Wisdom

wisdom and perfect health are inseparable buddies.

ACCESSING WISDOM

STEP ONE: Ten minutes of *The Atonement.*

STEP TWO: Isolate a present problem you'd like a wise solution to. Then think, "What is the highest wisdom for me to know about so and so?" The answer comes in your thoughts. Speak it out, and verify with your "Yes" and "No" tools that what you speak is indeed Truth. Only ask about present situations. Never delve into the future or past.

STEP THREE: Write in your journal the wisdom you receive.

CHAPTER SEVENTEEN

Knowledge From The Masters

You are swimming in a sea of wisdom. There is never any reason to be perplexed. You can know anything you need to know.

That is the key: *need to know.* If you buy a new computer, it comes with a manual that lays out all you need to know to operate it. It doesn't come with a manual for an air conditioner. If it did, the knowledge would be of no practical value. Even if you might find an air conditioner manual interesting, you'll only get one when you buy a unit and need to know how to operate it.

It is the same for the universe. You have access to the complete manual for your life. You don't have the manual to someone else's life. And you don't have the manual for a different time. The manual you have access to is for your life at this time on this planet. Anything and everything that pertains to that is available.

You access wisdom during The Atonement because your conscious connection to The Unified Field is open then. This doesn't mean you can't receive wisdom any other time. You can and do access it at all times. In fact, the plan is that you are forever immersed in knowledge. However, until your conscious awareness is permanently locked into The

Knowledge From The Masters

Unified Field, wisdom comes most easily during The Atonement.

When you ask questions during The Atonement, include in each question the words *"highest and wisest."* "Is it in my *highest and wisest* interest to do so and so?" Or, "What is the *highest and wisest* knowledge for me to know about so and so?" Or, "What is the *highest and wisest* activity for me to earn money?" *Highest and wisest* clearly denote your intention.

While you are receiving the answer, keep The Atonement Vibration with you. It is a safeguard that you are indeed connected to The Unified Field, and that the answer is highest wisdom.

In addition, always check the answer with the aid of the "Yes" and "No" tools. "Is what I have just spoken out the correct answer to my question?" If the answer is no, find out why not. It may be that this is not knowledge you need to know at this time. It may be the answer got garbled with erroneous input from your intellect.

Highest wisdom is concerned with restoring and maintaining balance and harmony. Any knowledge that helps do that is readily available. It can deal with any aspect in your life: relationships, career, recreation, health, and so on. Each facet of your life pushes and guides you to wholeness.

Be aware there may be more than one answer. For instance, if you ask for your highest and wisest course of action to make money, there may be many options, all of which are equally wise. Each step toward the goal could also have several options that may even be opposites. Always check for the other options. For instance, you might learn it is in your highest and wisest interest to change jobs. At the same time it

PART IV / The Rewards

might be in your highest and wisest interest not to change jobs. Either course is wise.

Accessing highest wisdom does not eliminate decisions. You can't use this as a substitute for consciously steering your own life. What it does do is narrow your options to those that are equally wise. Choosing one of them won't be a mistake. Then making decisions is fun. Gone is bewilderment and worry. Just choose the option that most appeals to you. It is like picking a beauty queen among fifteen finalists. A mistake can't be made.

You may ask questions that only need a Yes or No answer. If you do this, however, always ask if the opposite is also true. "It is in my highest and wisest interest to reconcile with Drew?" If you get a "yes", then ask, "Is it in my highest and wisest interest not to reconcile with Drew?" Remember, if you receive a "No", ask if it is a "true No" because "No" may not be the answer to your question. If it isn't, find out what the "No" means.

You can get a "No" answer when you've already asked this question and received the answer. Up to a point you can keep asking the same question if you feel uncertain. Sooner or later, however, you're going to have to accept the answer. When a question has been asked and answered enough, you'll just get a "No" answer, meaning, "No answer—the question has been asked and answered."

Where do these answers come from? Highest wisdom comes from only one source: The Unified Field. Your Self knows how to dip into that vat of pure knowledge, learn what it needs to know, then put it into language you understand. Your Self goes nowhere to find the vat, although

Knowledge From The Masters

sometimes it's easier to think it does. The vat is all around you. It underlies everything; it is the source of everything. There is no way to avoid it. Quite literally, you are now swimming in a sea of pure knowledge. Whenever you need wisdom, your expressed desire can attract the perfect answers instantly.

When you are consciously connected to The Unified Field, you constantly tap wisdom. The process never ends. If you are not consciously connected, you usually ignore the wisdom or don't hear it. Asking questions, getting answers, and then relying on the answers strengthens your conscious bond to The Unified Field, that source of All-Knowing Intelligence.

The implications for your health are far reaching. First, health must include the ability to access wisdom. If you aren't wise, something isn't working right. Perfect health means your systems are all functioning at peak capacity. They are doing what they are designed to do. Any system operating at reduced capacity is poor health.

If the heart pumps blood through clogged arteries, the circulatory system is operating at reduced capacity. That is poor health. If your channel to All-Knowing Intelligence is clogged so you don't hear highest wisdom, you think at reduced capacity. That is also poor health.

As part of the healing process, these techniques open your access to wisdom. They connect your thinking to The Unified Field for all the knowledge supporting your life. Some of the knowledge you receive is is bound to be how to reduce stress and improve your health. You can learn about your habits that need to be changed. Or you might learn you need to change your diet

PART IV / The Rewards

because your body's requirements have changed. You need never guess again about how to be healthy. You came stocked with knowledge. Now you know how to access it.

Everyone has the same connection to The Unified Field. That means everyone is connected to each other via The Unified Field.

Because of everyone's connection to everyone else, you can receive knowledge and guidance from an enlightened Master. This is nothing new. People have been receiving such guidance for eons.

The knowledge you can receive from a Master is the very same knowledge you can receive from your Self. However, the Master imparts a feeling of love that is unique to the Master. The feeling has healing qualities of its own because love is the great healer. Love melts away illusionary issues and problems. Love speeds recovery times and promotes spontaneous remissions. Indeed, love delivered piggyback on knowledge from a Master is mighty powerful!

The Master can be any person with or without a physical body that is consciously connected to The Unified Field. Some Masters live on earth working with people to assure the planetary transition. Most, however, reside at another layer of creation. All of the Masters are available to you.

Some Masters are identified with religions, such as Jesus, Moses, Abraham, Babaji, Mohammed, Buddha, and Krishna. Others are not so familiar. Like you, they are created in the image of Our Creator. Their message is to awaken people to their own Mastership. They continue relentlessly to open everyone's awareness to The Unified Field.

Knowledge From The Masters

    To connect with a Master, begin with ten minutes of The Atonement. Then ask for the vibration of a Master. The vibration is a movement, sensation, or vision that is pleasant. The name of the Master appears as a thought unless you specify a particular one. Open your awareness to the master's vibration, and feel the unique expression of love in your heart. The feeling is reward enough, but you can also ask questions. The procedure is identical to asking questions of your Self, and the answers are also identical.

    Write in your journal a description of each Master's vibration you receive. You might leave some space for other masters' vibrations as they come to you.

    When you communicate with a Master, you receive a peace of mind and a sense of unity with creation. This has profound health benefits. It melts away stress without a trace. Connecting with a Master is a dose of the most powerful tonic.

PART IV / The Rewards

CONNECTING WITH THE MASTERS

STEP ONE: Ten minutes of The Atonement.

STEP TWO: Think, "Give me a Master's Vibration." Notice a movement, sensation, or vision, and feel the Master's love. The name of the Master appears in your thoughts unless you specify a particular Master.

STEP THREE: Receive highest wisdom from the Master in the same way you receive highest wisdom from your Self.

STEP FOUR: Write in your journal a description of The Master's Vibration and a summary of the wisdom you receive.

Chapter Eighteen

Peace

Peace of mind is the end product of a healthy body. You can't find peace when you're sick. You can't find it under stress. You can't even find it with a nervous system that is operating at less than peak performance.

Many of the richest people in the world would willingly give their fortunes in exchange for feelings of peace. Some people spend a lifetime accumulating power, possessions, and leverage, only to find the greatest gift eludes them. Somehow they have the notion it is at the end of their rainbow—if only they could succeed in the world of finance, their world would be complete. Well, it isn't.

That is not to chastise money and financial gain. There is nothing wrong with abundance. In fact, it is one of the rewards of a stress-free life. Indeed it is a necessary ingredient for the full experience of life.

The problem with money has come not from having it, but from thinking it leads to peace of mind. "If only I could pay off these bills and get ahead, then I'd have peace," you may have thought at some time. But when the bills got paid and you did get money in the bank, did peace come? Only temporarily, if at all. Money is not the source of peace.

PART IV / The Rewards

It is so sad to see the world's wealthiest people in mental turmoil. On the surface they appear to have it all. Yet they are unhappy and tense. They bark at their closest friends. They growl at their spouses. They lament every little condition around them. All their wealth has bought them no peace of mind.

Why? How could that be? Because they missed the source for peace. It comes from a conscious connection to infinite silence—your old friend, The Unified Field. When your nervous system is operating at its healthiest, this connection is automatic. There is nothing to do. Nothing needs to be cultivated. No effort needs to be expended. Peace is just the normal, natural outgrowth of perfect health.

With that connection, the wealthy business person can experience the full rewards of achievement. To wallow in wealth with peace of mind is the intention of Our Creator. For either peace or wealth to be missing marks an unfulfilled life.

Your personal peace is guaranteed in the scheme of nature's plan. Peace is normal and natural. It is not a reward for working hard to find it. It is simply the reward for being in tune with love, with The Unified Field.

By now you know how simple that can be to achieve. Since the first moments of experiencing The Atonement, you have felt the waves of peace. The more entrenched becomes your conscious connection to The Unified Field, the more powerful and permanent becomes that peace.

Peace of mind is connected to physical health. To be free of illness yet in mental turmoil is still poor health. Few people realize peace of mind is related to their physical bodies. The experience

Peace

of peace requires a connection to The Unified Field. That requires a nervous system that can operate at a refined physical state. Therefore, to experience peace you must have the foundation of a healthy physical body. It is a prerequisite.

During The Atonement, you experience a greater sense of peace because you are consciously connected to The Unified Field. When you go back into activity, a myriad of challenges face you, so your nervous system refocuses on the projects at hand. The refocusing causes the feelings of peace to diminish.

They diminish, but something is retained. You don't return to the same turmoil or emptiness. Each time you do The Atonement, small permanent changes are made in your nervous system, such as mending broken tissue or chemical changes in brain fluid. Over time it becomes more and more able to sustain the conscious connection and the feelings of peace while it also engages in all kinds of other activities.

Each session of The Atonement produces some change. Each session brings a greater awareness of peace. Each session builds on past sessions, and the effects accumulate to lay the foundation for permanent peace of mind.

You can experience peace even as you rise to meet any challenge. To feel peace does not make you weak. You don't get less dynamic. You don't turn away from injustice. You don't give into inappropriate pressure. Never! Peace of mind makes you even more effective in combating injustice, hate, revenge, misplaced power, and evil. You become a dynamic advocate of order and fairness.

PART IV / The Rewards

Peace of mind allows you to accurately assess your world. When you come across a situation you know is wrong and you can help, peace of mind allows you to delve in with correct and measured response. With direction and power, you can truly help smooth out any difficulty.

You might even be forceful if that is required. However, infused with the force is peace. Peace and force are not opposites. They can and do exist side by side. To be open for peace does not mean giving up your dynamism. It means simply that you won't be overwhelmed. You act with force while maintaining equilibrium.

Religious documents are replete with stories about holy people rising to an occasion to make a point. None of these people had the spine of a wet towel. They were all powerful leaders with a conscious connection to The Unified Field and an overlay of peace in all their activities.

Yes, you can and should be concerned about the turmoil around you. You can be an activist for the environment, for human rights, for disarmament, for ending poverty, for animal rights, or whatever your cause. There are thousands of worthy projects, and each needs attention. Coming to grips with all the errors of human civilization is necessary, so don't let up on your concerns. You are much more valuable with peace of mind. You are many times more effective. Peace gives you direction, purpose, and wisdom.

As you infuse peace into your own life, you infuse it into mass consciousness. Everyone is connected, so when you experience the peace of The Unified Field, peace is felt to some degree by everyone else. There is a lasting effect.

Peace

Feeling peace is really feeling infinite orderliness, which is the foundation for nature. In The Unified Field there is no hint of chaos, turmoil, or confusion. That infinite order carries with it infinite power. An ounce of order can dissolve tons of disorder. And, since everyone is connected, your peace infects everyone to such a significance that world peace is the benefactor.

Yes, the peace you are developing in your own life even contributes to world peace. That is not an empty platitude. It is a fact. A few people developing inner peace by consciously connecting to The Unified Field do promote world peace. It only takes a handful of people to guarantee global transformation because of the power of orderliness.

This is already happening. Not long ago, the world seemed to be on the brink of nuclear disaster. Oppression was common. War and threats of war abounded all over the globe. All that is changing. To the amazement of all but the most aware, the world is becoming peaceful.

The aware are not surprised. In their own way, they have been instilling peace into mass-consciousness while cultivating it into their own lives. With regular personal techniques, they have been injecting order into the community of nations. It is no mere coincidence world leaders now refer to a "new world order."

You can not add greater dimension to your life than instilling inner peace from The Unified Field. At the same time you can't make a greater contribution to the world. Let peace spill into every experience you have and splash through mass-consciousness to touch every soul.

Peace—from your own quiet enjoyment to a new world order—peace is now inevitable.

CHAPTER NINETEEN

Abundance

You live in an abundant world. Nature is extravagant. She has created more plant and animal forms than mankind has been able to identify. Furthermore, they keep changing. They adapt to all the pressures people place on them, bending and correcting to survive the onslaught of pollution, destruction, and misuse.

Extravagance—even the perpetuation of extravagance—is the hallmark of Our Creator's Creation. Why then are so many people in this world starving? Why do so many people live without their basic needs taken care of? Why is there a struggle between the "haves" and the "have-nots"?

The answer is found in the stress of the people on this planet. Poverty is a stress symptom. It stems from poorly functioning nervous systems that aren't flowing with the natural abundance of nature. Simplistic? Yes! But true.

Every person on this planet is made in the image of Our Creator. That means every person is a creator. That means every person can create his and her own experiences, including the experience of abundance or of poverty.

The problem is not a lack of abundance. The earth is still overflowing with abundance, in spite of what mankind has done to destroy its

Abundance

bounty. The abundance is here. It is only a matter of tapping into it wisely.

At first blush the problem of world poverty seems extremely complicated. It appears to defy solution. Intertwined are issues of power, free trade, logistics, storage, international monetary systems, transportation, to mention a few. A genie couldn't sort out the problems, let alone begin to address all the questions posed. Conferences, blue ribbon committees, the United Nations, thousands of charities, and billions of dollars in government aid can't seem to come to grips with poverty.

Governments declare wars on poverty. They pump money into social programs. They ship food to famine areas. They provide education. Yet not a dent is made in poverty. Why? Because the solution can't be found in the problem.

Suppose cars had no lights and at night they kept running into each other, causing injury and death. Approaches to solve the problem might be to make rubber cars, to prohibit night driving, and to invent complicated automatic steering devices. Or the problem could be solved by adding headlights. Just turn on a light.

In one approach the problem is analyzed, but the darkness is retained. The other approach eliminates the basic problem of darkness by just turning on a headlight.

That is what you can do to receive abundance in life. Forget about your lack. Don't focus on the darkness to correct it. Instead turn on a light. The light is none other than The Unified Field. Making conscious contact with it brings into your life all the abundance of nature.

This is natural. Abundance is your natural condition. You only need to be in tune with the

PART IV / The Rewards

infinite. Then all of infinity flows to and through you.

When you reduce stress with these techniques, you must also experience abundance. Perfect health means a perfect flow of cosmic energies. It means a continuous flow of wealth. This is intended. This is the cosmic plan. This is your birthright.

When you are grounded in The Unified Field, you seek wealth for your well being and enjoyment, and you do not seek it for power over others, for ego aggrandizement, or for selfish pleasure. By your wealth the world is made a better place. Everyone is the beneficiary.

The way you gain wealth supports the highest good of everyone. What you do elevates you and everyone around you without harming nature or any person. When people learn to use the wealth of the cosmos in this way, abundance for everyone will never stop flowing.

You don't even have to be concerned about why you seek wealth. Your highest purposes are in your thoughts automatically when you are flowing with nature. Step by step the path to abundance unfolds. This is an automatic process. It comes as surely as the dawn follows the night.

You can adapt The Atonement to gain an even stronger grip on abundance. First, establish a goal, and make sure it is correct for you. This is done by asking during The Atonement, "What is a perfect goal or project for me to manifest wealth?" Use your "Yes" and "No" tools to verify the answer that comes in your thoughts.

Next, discover the first action you need to take to fulfill the goal. You might get several options, since there may be several equally wise courses

Abundance

of action. Choose the most appealing option, do what is called for, and move on to the next action you need to take. This is easy and logical. It is simply using your expanded awareness to find the best goal or project, then to follow the most efficient set of actions that take you to the goal.

Write in your journal the goal and actions you take to fulfill the goal. When the goal is reached, enter the success with ink of your favorite color.

Efficiency is the key. Everything that flows with nature is efficient. Nature expends the least energy to accomplish maximum results. When you are flowing with nature, you are just as efficient.

With such efficiency, with powerful goals that are perfect for you, and with clear direction on the course of action to fulfill the goals, you can't go wrong. That is perfected skill. There is nothing you can't do. The reward is free-flowing abundance. Such a wonderful adjunct to perfect health!

PART IV / The Rewards

MANIFESTING WEALTH

STEP ONE: Ten minutes of The Atonement.

STEP TWO: Ask, "What is a perfect project or goal for me to manifest wealth?" The answer comes in your thoughts. Verify with your "Yes" and "No" tools. If you have a specific project or goal in mind, verify in the same way that it is perfect for you.

STEP THREE: Ask, "What is an action I need to take to accomplish my goal?" The answer comes in your thoughts, and you may receive several options. Verify the options with your "Yes" and "No" tools.

STEP FOUR: Pick the most appealing option and do the action called for.

STEP FIVE: Repeat steps three and four until the goal is reached.

STEP SIX: Write in your journal the goal, and the actions you take to fulfill the goal. When the goal is reached, enter the success with ink of your favorite color.

CHAPTER TWENTY

Ideal Relationships

Ideal relationships are rooted in your physiology. A whole, perfectly functioning nervous system is a prerequisite for lasting meaningful people in your life. Without stress-free health, you simply can not feel the essence of another soul.

Ideal relationships boil down to one simple fact: the easier it is for you to feel love, the easier it is for you to relate to others. It is simply a matter of developing the ability to feel love.

And you know what this love you feel is. It is The Unified Field. It is the most basic, most elementary, most fundamental level of creation. Everything in all of creation is created with The Unified Field. When you tap into it with The Atonement, you stir your own feelings of love.

You are of course always surrounded by The Unified Field, but you must stir it to feel it as love. It is like lying in a warm bath. Only when you move do you feel its warmth, even though the warm water is all around you.

Religious people from all faiths say God is love. Indeed, that is Truth. Our Creator is The Unified Field—love. When you touch The Unified Field with The Atonement, or countless other paths, you consciously connect to Our Creator. Like stirring in warm bath water, you feel the

PART IV / The Rewards

presence of Our Creator into whom you are always immersed. What you feel is love.

Feeling love all the time is in your blueprint. You are created to be aware of Our Creator and the connection you have to all the rest of creation. The awareness is experienced as love.

When you do The Atonement and dip into The Unified Field, you probably don't think of your connections and ties to everyone. Nevertheless, some part of you does fathom the whole picture. That part is awe struck with the beauty, complexity, yet simplicity of creation that gets unveiled. Like a child being presented with a giant chocolate sundae, your soul leaps in wonder as feelings of love spring up.

When your connection to everyone and everything is revealed to your innermost nature, you are never the same again. Without realizing why, you view everything and everyone with a reverence. They are appreciated the same way you appreciate your own arm—that is, as an aspect of your Self. Nothing appears foreign or outside. All is to be protected and never to be harmed. A benevolence replaces indifference and hostility.

The longer you do these techniques, the greater is your appreciation of that connection. The blueprint for creation is not a secret. It is for you to know, and each time you do The Atonement, you gain insight and knowledge. It just takes time for body healing and restructuring to realize your connection to everyone and everything.

Can't you imagine what this new perception means in your everyday dealings with people? Can't you imagine what the world will be like when everyone has this view? What would

Ideal Relationships

happen to crime? And Wars? And hate? Revenge? Oppression? Greed?

Don't these stem from the erroneous belief that each person is an island? Only the insane would harm himself, or declare war on himself, or hate himself. Only the insane with delusions about himself could inflict intentional injury. Yet that is what people's actions toward each other boil down to. It is insane.

Insanity is the illness of this time, but it is coming to an end. The technology is here to grasp Truth to understand the problem and inoculate everyone with The Unified Field.

The inoculation can't help but improve all your relationships. Furthermore, you can't feel love in your heart without it splashing all over the place. Everyone you meet gets "wet" by this splash. They feel love just by your presence. And they respond to you in the same way—with love. This is inevitable.

Relationships are many and varied. Some people come into your life to help in business. Some come to play games with you. Some special souls come into your life to form a family. Whatever reason someone comes into your life, these techniques assure a successful bond with him or her.

The Atonement Vibration by itself gives you relationship support. However, when special attention needs to be focused on a relationship, you can magnify the effects with a Relationship Vibration. Perhaps you really want to locate a perfect lover, if that is in your highest and wisest interest. Or perhaps you need to bring partners into your business. Or perhaps you moved to a new city and you are mustering a support group.

PART IV / The Rewards

These are the kind of needs that can be helped with The Relationship Vibration.

Once you discover it, just allow it to be in your awareness the second half of The Atonement. This technique facilitates an easy flow of people through your life. It sets up a kind of protective shield around you, only letting in the most useful people. It also fends off those who may harm you.

To discover The Relationship Vibration, begin with ten minutes of The Atonement. Then think, "Give me The Relationship Vibration." It could be any movement, sensation, or vision that is comfortable and easily noticed—the same criteria as for all the other vibrations. When it comes, verify with the aid of your "Yes" and "No" tools.

Describe The Relationship Vibration in your journal. Also keep an account of any situations that are helped with this technique.

You can also guarantee that the right people come into your life by freely asking questions during The Atonement. For instance, if you want to know if someone is a perfect business partner, ask, "Is it in my highest and wisest interest to go into business now with so and so?" And always ask the opposite: "Is it in my highest and wisest interest not to go into business now with so and so?" This may be a situation where you have opposite options, both being in your highest and wisest interest.

Keep in mind that answers only deal with what to think at the *present* time. They won't reveal the future. So, if you want to find out if Drew is your perfect lover, you'll only learn what is in your highest and wisest interest to think for the present time. If the answer is yes, that may

Ideal Relationships

not preclude many others from also being your perfect lover.

Whenever you're asking about someone else, keep in mind the doctrines of privacy and freewill. You can never invade someone's thoughts and get information they aren't willing to give. And you can never steal their freewill to decide their fate. That is precisely why you can only learn what it is best for you to think at the present moment. You can think what appears to be unfolding presently, but someone's actions could completely change the course of events.

There is no reason now why you can't have ideal relationships. Always. Without exception. Just stay regular with The Atonement and everything else falls into place. Freedom from stress and ideal relationships go hand in hand.

THE RELATIONSHIP VIBRATION

STEP ONE: Ten minutes of The Atonement.

STEP TWO: Think, "Give me a Relationship Vibration." It comes as a vibration somewhere, a movement of the body, a sensation, a vision, or anything pleasant that can be noticed. Verify with your "Yes" and "No" tools.

STEP THREE: Use The Relationship Vibration during the second ten minutes of The Atonement when you are faced with issues in your life about relationships or need guidance to a particular kind of person.

STEP FOUR: Describe The Relationship Vibration in your journal. Also keep an account of all situations that are helped with this technique.

Chapter Twenty One

Happiness

Happiness is. It just is. You may think you are happy because.... Or because.... Or because.... Fill in nearly anything. A good feeling that arises when something special happens too often is what is meant by "happiness."

Happiness is. It just is. It doesn't have to have a reason. Happiness is the feeling everyone is made to feel all the time. The only requirement is that you are consciously connected to The Unified Field.

If you're not consciously connected to The Unified Field, you don't feel happiness, and a void results. The natural response is to look for things that make you feel good. Those things then become all-important. Without them you aren't "happy." Cars, winnings, surprises, gadgets, chocolate, job promotions, raises, sex, and so the list goes.

These things are not bad. They are part of a productive and satisfying life. However, to give them the power of happiness misses the mark. They can give pleasure and make you feel good, but they should be no more than ripples on a deep ocean of happiness that always is.

The feelings of happiness and the feelings of love are two flavors of the same ecstasy. Both are what The Unified Field feels like. Both verify

Happiness

your connection to your source. Both come from feeling Our Creator. Both need neither an object nor a reason. Both just are. Both are yours because you are created in the image of Our Creator. Both are always present and overlay all emotions and all experiences. Both are your birthright.

The feelings of happiness are the feelings of perfect health. There is no way you can have perfect health without a never-ending bath in happiness. It is impossible. When your nervous system functions as it is designed to function, it naturally generates the feelings of happiness.

Conversely, the feelings of happiness usher in perfect health. Scientific studies point that out. A person's happy outlook has significant bearing on every cell in the body.

Happiness does not deprive anyone of the full range of human emotions. Because the fleeting feelings of pleasure from our things play themselves out, people have the idea that happiness must be temporary. They can't conceive of a never-ending feeling of happiness underlying all their emotions, even sadness and grief.

Well, happiness can exist along side all your emotions because true happiness is not an emotion. Happiness only comes with feeling your conscious connection to The Unified Field, and happiness is independent of everything else. You can feel sadness and grief, but you experience with them an awareness of the broad picture, the purpose, and the perfection of life. Underneath is the clear reminder that you are also happy regardless of what is going on in your life.

PART IV / The Rewards

There is nothing that gives greater perspective or a more solid foundation in life than happiness. With it comes power. No doubt you've noticed how much more productive happy people are. For the enlightened person, happiness comes first, then stunning accomplishment. Lives with successes piled upon successes are grounded in happiness.

Happiness is the foundation of leadership. After all, what is really doing the leading? The Unified Field is at the helm, guiding and directing. What a position of strength for any leader! With happiness in your periscope, your ship is bound to take the lead and guide others to their destination.

Happiness is the end product for which people do everything. Hardly an action is performed without hoping it will bring a bit more happiness. The Truth is that happiness is far simpler to find than doing one thing, then another, and yet another. Happiness comes naturally with any practice that opens your awareness to The Unified Field.

You now have the secret that has eluded so many. Share it.

Chapter Twenty Two

Light

Some people shine from within. Others have a dark cloud around them. The more conscious your connection to The Unified Field, the brighter you shine. The healthier you are, the brighter you shine. The less stress you have, the brighter you shine.

Light comes from The Unified Field so everyone is light. The difference is the luster. You are already light, but you may have the rheostat turned way down.

The light some people emanate is a beacon. Everyone sees it, but they aren't sure what they see. "He has a presence." "She shines." "Your eyes sparkle." "He radiates peace."

Light from The Unified Field shines forth from your body. Celestial eyes see it. Physical eyes notice something. The light is a reminder to everyone to come home to their source. They subconsciously hear the call.

You've experienced the shining light of enlightened souls. They do not need to say anything to illuminate Truth. Their presence says it all.

You are such a light when you are consciously connected to The Unified Field. Quite innocently, you become an advocate for Truth without uttering a sound.

PART IV / The Rewards

Perfect health is your gift to yourself with the regular practice of these techniques. Light is the gift you give to humanity.

When enough people are enlightened, darkness will find no place to hide on this planet. Every corner and every soul will hear the call home. That's actually why so many seemingly lost souls are here now. Some part of them knows what's happening here, and they want in on it.

Of course many will refuse to heed the call. That is their freewill, and their choice will be respected. They are made no less perfect for their decision, and they remain in the image of Our Creator. At some other time and in some other place they too will consciously realize their connection to their source.

Light is neither something you cultivate, nor generate, nor perfect. Light is a natural aspect of perfect health. There is no way you can eliminate stress without also becoming a beacon of light. As a radiator of light you elevate consciousness of humankind by your mere presence.

CHAPTER TWENTY THREE

Your Journal Of Truth

To have perfect health is to experience "Your Attributes." They surface when you consciously realize your connection to The Unified Field. Each attribute appears without fanfare, without effort, and without conditions. They are part of your make-up.

You don't have to cultivate "Your Attributes." You don't have to go through a myriad of lessons. All "Your Attributes" become obvious when the whole you is opened up.

These techniques are one path to realizing the wholeness you are. This is not the only path. It may not even be the best path for you. However, if you've come this far in this book, let that be your clue.

Just reading this book enlivens The Unified Field to some degree. However, to fully awaken The Unified Field and assure perfect health, you must regularly practice the techniques.

In these pages you have been exposed to only a few of "Your Attributes," but you now have the skill to learn about others. In fact, you can learn Truth about all aspects of creation. You can tap into All-Knowing Intelligence.

Invest in a beautiful new journal to write Truth in. This Journal Of Truth is to be your bible. All you need to know about any aspect of

PART IV / The Rewards

life will come to you to fill its pages. Much of what you write you will share. Much will be meaningful for you alone. All of it will be golden wisdom to illumine your understanding of life.

The procedure to fill up your Journal Of Truth is straight forward. After ten minutes of The Atonement, ask "What Truth is appropriate for me to write in my journal at this time?" Open your eyes and write in the journal the thoughts that come to you. Periodically, verify with your "Yes" and "No" tools that you are indeed writing Truth. After ten minutes or so, close your eyes for awhile and come out slowly in the usual way to avoid roughness or irritation.

This is your Journal of Truth for any subject that tickles your fancy. Never again do you need rely on what others have written. You are a conduit of knowledge that is perfect for you to have now.

Keep in mind that Truth is a strange concept. Like time, it seems to be exact, but it isn't. What is Truth for one person may not be Truth for another. That's why you must respect what other people think without judging them or their ideas.

Truth may be different in different states of consciousness. As you become more conscious of your connection to The Unified Field, you will see doctrines of Truth change. What you hold as Truth at a certain time is perfect for you at that time and in that state of consciousness. As you awaken, your knowledge of Truth changes.

That is why you alone need to be your own conveyor of Truth. Rely on no-one. When you look to anyone for Truth, you accept their level of consciousness. Do that no longer. You are

Your Journal Of Truth

now your own guru. Your Journal Of Truth is the highest reward from these techniques.

Run now with the person you are. Accept your perfect health. Accept freedom from stress. Accept "Your Attributes." And accept the Master you have always been.

THE JOURNAL OF TRUTH

STEP ONE: Ten minutes of The Atonement.

STEP TWO: Think, "What Truth is appropriate for me to write in my journal at this time?" Listen to the answer in your thoughts.

STEP THREE: Open your eyes and write in your Journal Of Truth knowledge that comes to you. Verify periodically with your "Yes" and "No" tools that you are indeed writing Truth.

STEP FOUR: Close your eyes for a couple of minutes, and come out slowly to avoid roughness or irritation.